The Anatomy of Significance

The Answer To Matter and Meaning

*The Question of Relationships is Evolutionary.
Where there is Evolution, there is no Answer,
only what's Next...*

Milton Howard, Jr.

The Anatomy of Significance

Copyright © 2014 by Milton Howard, Jr.

All rights reserved. No part of this book may be reproduced or transmitted in any form or by any means without written permission of the author.

ISBN 978-1499321395

Table of Contents

Resolving the Question of Relationships 1

What I Want is Priority #1	1
Desire and Relationship	2
Growing Dark	4
Response Ability	7
The New Us	9
Give an Account	11
The Answer to Matter and Meaning	13
The Anatomy of Time	16
Intimacy and Timing	18
Strategies for Significance	25
The Gift of Pushing	27

The Law of Accounting 29

The Mind Body	13
The Anatomy of Memory	36
Deciding What You Want	38
Choosing Your Line of Site	43
The Trees of Life	49
The Emotional Body	55
The Substance of Sound	58
The Relationship Accounts Body	63
Intimate Action and Integrity	68
Closing the Distance	69
The Time Body - Your Outer Mirror	73
Frequency and Time	75
The Sound of Time	77
Spirit Body - Your Inner Mirror	82
The Energy Body	83
The Universal Response Body	84
Your Completions Body	84

Rules of Engagement 88

The Gift of Measurement   94

        Measured Motifs   95
        Measured Money   96
        Measures Moments   96

The 12 Points of Significance   97

        Measured Monuments   106

Universal Parenting Energy 107

        Practice Your Personal Frequencies   111
        Sex, Is it Good for Business?   112
        The Luxury of Touch   113
        The Gift of Attention   113
        The Maturing of Connections   115
        Opening Up from the Cutoff   119

Resolving the Question of Relationships

Chapter 1

Resolving The Question of Relationship

What would be your response if I told you that I could make it to where you will never feel empty again? The word "empty" is a description used to describe one of the most daunting states of emotion that anyone can feel, but the word "empty" is only a description of what one would say that they "feel" within their body as it concerns insignificance. Using the word "empty" here is a wrong word assignment. If I could take and replace the word "empty" with the word "distant" or "distance", we would more accurately acquire a better description of the actual condition of what one is experiencing. This leads to a more accessible solution to the problem of significance by using the word "distant" or "distance". So here, we are not filling a hole, but closing a distance. Distance is at the core of insignificance and your relationships are at the core of distance, but we misplace the purpose and priority of our relationships. To resolve the issue of insignificance we must switch priorities. Although our sense of significance comes from our relationships, it is prioritizing what you want in life that becomes the solution.

What I Want, Priority #1

The single most important human possession is desire. Yes, to want something. Some spiritual enthusiast would downplay this notion by valuing the idea of a life without possessions, which are generally based on desire, is somehow a more spiritual state to be attained. But without desire, existence wouldn't exist. You have every right to want things. True life is to want something and then to get it, but most human beings fail to master this very process.

When a baby is born, it is born without a significant amount of human skill. It's alive, but the only attribute a newborn has is to want something. At a certain point, it wants to get out of the womb to be born into the world. Then it wants to breath. Then it wants to eat. It wants to be held. It wants to be nurtured. The beginning of life is about wanting. With this being the case, there are a myriad of people responding to the wants of the newborn, carrying within themselves a consciousness of the newborn's desires. So there is an immediate schematic set up here. This schematic is the bond that exists between desire and the resulting responsive relationships to that desire. There is a definite bond between desire and the relationships associated to that desire.

The beginning of life is about wanting.

At some point those initial relationships begin to wane for one reason or the other. At this point a chemical shoots out into the baby's body that gives it a sense that it is missing something, and the baby cries out in order to connect to those familiar known responses from those who initially carried a consciousness of the newborn's desire. As the child grows older, he or she will soon begin to get an unusual and strange response called "No". At this point it must be pondered and considered by the child, "what does this mean?". "What I desire is not coming, but more importantly someone has specifically decided not to give it to me". Herein lies the birth of the question of significance, the question of emptiness, or better yet a distance from desire because somebody didn't come through.

Desire and Relationship

Herein also lies the key to the most incredible pairing of ideals in existence. Desire and relationship. For every desire, there should be a relationship created that is consistent with that desire and parallel to that desire. What's killing many individuals today is their inability to tie significant relationships to their desire. We know how to have desires, but we don't know how to build adequate relationships that relate to our desires. Most people are therefore left in a state of insignificance, not realizing that there is a fixed coexistence between desire and relationship. What people do is to simply relate to others apart from their desire. So most people just assume that there is something wrong with their desire, but never check the personages they are associated with. Some even stop desiring.

I'm going to throw something at you here that will take some mental strength to swallow and will take even a bit more to digest. No person or no individual should ever be your end goal, the object of your desire, nor set as the aim of your aspiration. You cannot make a person a target or a point of accomplishment. A person should never be something that you go after. "I want this person or that person" is an erroneous thought process that can only create phantom existences. Trust me. It will confuse your body. I will explain this later as we learn a little bit more about the chemicals of emotion.

Check this out. You cannot "accomplish" a person no matter how hard you try. With this, you cannot direct your desires towards a person or a relationship. This is not the place for desire, but your relationships should be a place for expectation. Let me explain.

The order is to have a tangible desire first and then to form relationship second based on that desire. You must first set a point of aspiration, and then create a relationship or a series of relationships around that. This notion, if properly understood would close almost every psychologist office and shut down at least 50% of churches. When one moves to try to make a relationship work, he or she will constantly be all over the place, trying to pin down perfection, but everything will remain elusive. The human heart is designed to desire. Desire what? Things. To misplace this core desire into a relationship will send you into an eternal black hole. So for a minute, let's try this and not be scared of the possibilities under this model or mode of existence.

Let's place desire on things and then place expectations on relationships. This order becomes the procurement of true love and for true love. Love established here is greater than a phantom love established through chasing an individual. Imagine someone loving what you want or loving what you are aspiring to. With this comes the natural progression towards investment. To say I love you in any other way is not love. It is this investment of action towards who you are as it relates to the things you want that causes the right chemicals to flow within your body that will leave you in a true state of significance.

**Let's place desire on things and
then place expectations on relationships.**

Just in case you might think I am stupid, let's look at this from the Christian point of view within the first texts in the Bible. God made things first, and then He made man. Check out the level of intelligence that is established here. The relationship between God and man was for man to contribute and expand things. Desire came first. Relationship came second. Also look close when it was said, Let Us make man...we find the word "Us", a "relationship" was the foundation for accomplishment and not the accomplishment within itself. Relationships are reflective of God, and then the purpose of relationship was to be fruitful, create results, and to multiply. See, most people make the relationship the end result, thusly make the relationship within itself as something to be chased after, therefore the sense of love becomes distant, especially when people change-up on you no matter how much you "love" them or show them love.

Relationship is the foundation of accomplishment.

So I'll cut straight to the chase and then through the chase. Give your desires credence, and only then connect with those who can see you through your desires.

Growing Dark

The worst feeling in the world that a person can experience and the worst state of existence in the world that a person can experience is the feeling of insignificance. Insignificance is responsible for most of the dark times in our lives. Insignificance is responsible for suicide, relationship breakups, and the majority of depression. Actually insignificance is the source for most depressive states. Everybody suffers from dark times, and everybody runs across the issue of insignificance within his or her life at some point. A great number of people find it hard to deal with the subject of insignificance in which a whole economy is derived to address this one state of existence. People look for the assistance of doctors, psychologists, clergy, counselors, and even self-help gurus to deal with the feeling of insignificance.

Insignificance also finds itself as the source of a physical health crisis worldwide. How you feel inside affects your personal health. The history of insignificance shares a common history with separation and separation anxiety. No one ever wants to feel alone. No one ever wants to feel abandoned. No one ever wants to feel left out. Herein we find why insignificance exists; insignificance is a follow up to how relationships pan out within a person's life. It is a follow up or a result of the condition of one's relationships.

I always state that there is no such thing as self-esteem. I am a firm believer that the entirety of a person's self-esteem stems from the investments of others into one's own life. Yes you can self motivate, but the entirety of esteem comes from the investment of others into your life. So when we deal with the subject of insignificance, we are also dealing with the parallel subject of personal investments that come from others. But what we don't find here is an ability to measure these personal investments. So what makes us feel life or feel alive generally goes unchecked. People do anything to feel and gain significance, but find themselves feeling bad based on other's actions and reactions, based on others responses, and the level of attention they might receive.

There is no such thing as self-esteem.

Many people find themselves allowing behavior patterns towards them to come in without close monitoring or notice. This leaves entirety of one's personal health and psychological health at risk because no one can control what another person does. But you will find that you can control what you decide to accept into your life. This acceptance becomes vital, because it not only affects your personal health, but it also affects the health of all of your outer existences. So you don't just suffer from the inside, the suffering grows within the monumental existences growing outside of you from within. It is then that the state of insignificance can become a powerful force as it concerns your ability to live, move, and have your being.

You can control what you decide to accept into your life.

The state of insignificance can be paralyzing. Insignificance can interrupt with ease any normal state of living. Insignificance can tear at the core of your soul while you wonder why things, when it comes to people and your personal relationships are not what you want them to be. You can even become attached to the person who is the source of causing you to feel insignificant and repeat a poor sorrowful existence or an event over and over again. Some try to fill the black hole of insignificance with drugs, alcohol, and other addictions in order to bear the pain of deficient recognition and insufficient attention.

Some depend on religious sources and other spiritual institutions to resolve the issue of insignificance. They are told that God will fill that space, but in most cases they only find temporary relief and then cycle right back into a state of insignificance. For those who go to church on Sunday morning, this usually happens before Monday shows up. Why do you think people have to keep going back?

In life, one can only be authenticated by another. Self-authentication is an erroneous concept much like believing a retail store can exist without customers. It's like believing that we can get our bodily nutrition without eating. In much the same way, the nutrition of our psychological health comes from the diet that we partake of that extends from what other people bring to our table. Yes. You have a psychosomatic table and others are serving you at all times. Have you stopped lately and really paid attention to what's being brought to your table of life. It's pretty serious.

When one reaches the point of insignificance, he or she must now gain a consciousness and an acute awareness of what others around them are doing. How are they relating to you? What investments are people making into you? How are you being treated? What does someone bring to the table as it concerns your dream? None of this can be taken for granted. At the core of these questions is the consequence of your significance.

You must gain a consciousness and an acute awareness of what others around you are doing.

How someone feels about you is felt by you. It can leave you in the darkest moment of life, or it can leave you in the most ecstatic moment of life. Even strangers contribute to your significance. How a person feels about you is highly impactful. So what undergirds your significance is how you conduct your relationships. This includes romantic relationships, business relationships, platonic relationships, familiar relationships or any type of exchange when it comes to others.

Significance can be right in your life and it is not left up to random forces as to how you feel. People feel sorry for themselves, but if you think about it, it makes absolutely no sense. Feeling sorry stems from the lack of knowledge that you have power. The old adage states that knowledge is power. What it is, is that most people don't know. Most people don't know that significance is an intricate part of their existence. I would go as far to say that significance is not a result, but it is our existence. It is how we decide to exist within the world, and then added in, how people respond that existence.

People's responses to you become you! So now you must become responsible in managing responses. If you don't, you will end up feeling like crap in the end. This is because you become the definition of how you allow people to treat you and how you allow people to exchange with you.

People's responses to you become you!

Responsibility

With relationships being the subject of significance or insignificance, herein stands a forced responsibility. Your body is made up of a series of glands that secrete fluids. These secretions are actually responses to activity that are undergirded by your exchange with others. These fluids are the basis of your feelings which most consider to be our emotional system. Depending on how certain glands secrete these fluids, the response of these secretions build a chemical house within your body that represent the state of your relationships. With the impact of this being a fact of reality you must closely guard how people make you feel, and you must also guard the investments of others into yourself.

If you are a religious person, you must also be careful of making God more important than yourself when God has created you to be more important than Him. There is nothing worse than self-proclaimed insignificance in order to appease a God who you would think needs to be appeased in that way. The very nature of creation and where mankind stands within creative existence proves that mankind himself is the crowning point of all existence. We are to reflect who God is and not appease a God who is supposedly greater than you and I. This leaves us with the notion of allowing people to be more important than one self in order to get the attention of the other. This type of religious notion is reflected into how one runs his or her personal relationships and turns out to be an entire mess, leaving a whole segment of earth's population feeling insignificant. God's aim is for all to be great. He has provided the entirety of creation as a contribution to your greatness and then said, do things better than me.

So what should be our aim towards one another?

Our responsibility to this notion is profound. We must also be careful not to have a diminished capacity towards our investments towards one another as well as the investments we receive. Everything we say or do creates value, especially when it comes to another person. What we say and how we act towards another is immediately constructed within a person's body by the secretions of these glands that are designed to do just that, respond to your thoughts and behavior towards another.

Everything we say or do creates value.

You also build your feelings based on how someone responds to you. People's thoughts towards you are the construction materials that build your "feelings". But most don't even know or have an inkling of an idea that this can be managed even if you have spent a lifetime of being mistreated. It can be managed even if you had parents or loved ones who ignored you and your needs. It can be managed even if you have a husband or a wife who doesn't make you feel incredible. It can be managed even when your boss or co-workers never recognize your true value.

Your feelings can be managed and must be managed.

The height of human existence is found between what takes place between two or more people. All of our potential, production, progression, and power exist within this space. Without the "other", life ceases to exist. So to be responsible towards life clearly means that we must be responsible within our relationships. Whenever you have a desire or a dream, the next step is to manage the relationships according to that. Hope has no place in how people treat you. Never hope for things to turn out right with the "other". Make it right!

The New Us

Yes. This is a book on relationships. A book designed to help you find your significance. Finding purpose is one thing, but finding your significance is an entirely different subject. Purpose is related to direction. Significance is related to desire. More so, significance is related to how someone responds to your desire. Let me be clear here, I do not want to parse words. The entirety of the subject of significance hangs its hat on your desire and how people respond and relate to that desire.

Significance is related to how someone responds to your desire.

As anyone would say without question, relationships are vital to our existence. It is how we feel. It is how we close the distance to our desire. Life is just not about existence; life is about the responses to your existence. Your emotions are hinged on how your existence is responded to. Your emotions are also constructed by how you respond to people, places, and things. It is the entirety of these responses that is the definition of life itself. Life is not only an existence, but life is a response.

From the earliest life forms at the beginning of time, life pushes. The push of life only becomes valuable when there is a response to that push. It is the push and the response to the push that creates relationship. If in the beginning, had God said, and then nothing happened, God himself would have felt horrible. In the same light, as evolution progresses from the earliest stages of life, relationship has always been pivotal towards anything that exists. The entirety of life springs from relationship. From every religious persuasion and virtually every belief system, the story is the same; life extends from life. Without relationship this extension would be entirely impossible.

Some would say a bad diet or practices such as smoking, illicit use of drugs, non-exercise, and the like is the source of our diseases. But I would say that all diseases extends from diminished relationships that report immediately to the body it's state of existence. Heart attacks come from insignificance. Strokes come from insignificance. Cancer comes from insignificance. High blood pressure comes from insignificance. The body is an immaculate system of secretions that are constantly responding to instruction. Non-health can be secreted via hormones just as well as health, but these notions of the secretions come from our exchanges between one another, which is highly economic in nature.

Yes! People can and will make you sick.

Over evolutionary history, the parameters of relationship have matured as well as what I call the containers of relationships. Our physical bodies are only a response-container that exists within life, but it is not life itself. Within all physicality is energy, and energy is constantly exchanged. As life advanced over evolutionary time, so have the skills and inner workings of relationships advanced. What is important to note here is that we have not reached full potential when it comes to relationships. How we relate with one another as human beings is still advancing. Springing from the context of relationship is all of life, so if life is constantly advancing, the relationships continue to advance, which gives us constant and consistent higher forms of existing.

Any third world country that has progressed into a current economic super power, this progression has always been proceeded by a change in interpersonal relationships within that country, or an advancement in how the populous related with one another. Once the state of relationships advanced, then there was a gaining of advanced knowledge and technologies. As the relationships matured, so has the country. Even as mankind advanced out of earlier ages of primal existences, at each age, there was a maturation of relationships.

So tomorrow, there will be a new us as evolutionary history has proved throughout many stage of human existence. So tomorrow, we would have a better grasp and a newer understanding of how one can invest into the other in order to maintain ongoing significance. We have to step up in order to continue to evolve into higher heights of existence.

We must grow in order to eliminate the insecurity that individual's experience that affects their bottom line.

Significance is how we feel that tells us that we are alive. How does one experience his or her own aliveness? In this book we hope to give you some clues and strategies on making this happen. It is important to know that when your significance is intact, it gives you the power to not only relate better to those you love, but you will also gain the natural securities that you need in life which includes true wealth and attention. From the standpoint of significance one can advance without limitation to acclaim all the desires of their heart.

What stalls one's dream almost single-handedly is insignificance. Today that will change.

Give an Account

Numbers govern everything in life. As matter of fact you can consider everything in life as numbers. From the beginning of evolutionary time to now, numbers change. The difference between the very beginning of life to where we are now is just a number. Think about it, the difference between a shack and a multimillion-dollar home is just a number. Your body is a system of numbers. Normalized blood pressure is 120/80, a number. Your body temperature is a number we should be around 98.6°. Your weight and size is a number. Your vision is a number. It should be 20/20. When you measure your brain activity via an EEG machine, numbers are read as frequencies. Your cholesterol level is a number, which should be around 200 mg/dl. Your blood sugar level is a number. Normalized blood sugar levels should be between 60 mg/dl and 120 mg/ml. These are just a few things in your body that's governed by numbers. When things go bad it simply means that the numbers have shifted.

The whole of our economy is measured by numbers. You have the gross national product, interest rates, employment rates, the national debt level and the like, all governed by numbers. What determines whether something is good or bad is all based on the numbers. Numbers govern the value of the TVs that we watch. You have a small 19 inch TV and then you have a large 60 inch TV. The difference is just a number. The numbers shifts value and meaning is assigned. Again, a number governs the difference in a small house and a big house. In actuality, when a house is drawn up on a paper, the value of the paper is the same, but what shows up on the paper crafted by an architect is just a different set of numbers. The measurements, which are determined by numbers are translated by a general contractor, then by those who construct the house.

The rule is numbers are governed by cycles. Cycles are governed by intent and intent is governed by relationships. And guess what? You govern all relationships.

Where you start with relationships is where you end up with the numbers.

Any result in your life is usually measured and determine by a number. When you take a test, numbers determines your grade. When you get a job, a financial number determines the value of that job. If you're running a business, the success of that business is determined by wealth, which is simply a number. To achieve desired numbers takes a series of relationships that pushes intent within prescribed cycles that gives you a desired end result. Relationships determine your end result. Better stated, your relationships are your end results. Herein is the magic, where you start with relationships is where you end up with the numbers. You don't need a crystal ball and you don't need to call a psychic. You don't need to consult your pastor or hire a psychologist, generally when the relationship is not right the end result is not going to be what you want.

The Answer to Matter and Meaning

Meaning arises out of intimacy. Here intimacy becomes a matter of ability, so I want to start with this; sex and sexuality models the inner workings of how the Universe works, thusly it becomes the determinant of what something means. When I say intimacy, I am talking about connection, more so, how one connects.

Everyone wants his or her life to matter. Everyone wants his or her life to have meaning and purpose. Meaning and purpose can only rise out of connection or how you connect, and as far as connection is concerned, you must have active agreement with someone else. You can determine in your own mind that something has a particular meaning, but if that meaning is not activated within another's observation in terms of agreement, then meaning can't exist.

Ok. Let's go a little deeper, but I am going to switch the word meaning with the word purpose. No one can feel their purpose without another observing and saying, "Yes, you are that". All purpose must be authenticated by someone actively agreeing with you. Otherwise, life has no meaning. When I say actively agreeing, here, I am talking about how someone agrees. A person must agree on an intimate level in order for true meaning to arise. What happens here at this point is that people generally don't pay attention to their agreements that surround them thusly losing their sense of purpose.

Who in your life agrees with your purpose?

Let's purposefully go a little deeper. You and I are primarily a mass of energy. Most people think in terms of life as physical life. The word "physical" is just a term. If I can for a moment direct your attention to the concept of life as being energetic and not physical. When you talk about the "physical" you are really talking about energy. Pure energy.

Matter

As scientist are now discovering, there is really no such thing as matter. The deeper you go and the more you look as you go deeper, there is on only space. With this, I am going to throw a new term at you that you can make a part of your vocabulary and conversations:

Infinite Density…the deeper you go in terms of researching matter, you would think you would keep finding what one might consider more matter, but you will only find more space. This can go on into infinity. So there is really no such thing as physical matter, only what matters – meaning. Meaning can be considered here as the movement of matter. Matter, scientifically is how space moves and space only moves when there is agreement.

Let's go back to this; active agreements. Energy is always a result of agreement. Energy is movement. Nothing moves without agreement. What you must pay attention to is how the energies around you connect with you. Anyone would want their life to have meaning and purpose, but most are not acutely aware of their energy and how their energy is exchanging within their personal space.

Energy is always a result of agreement.
So pay attention to your agreements.

Here we have to go a little deeper, but it's not intentional. I really want you to get this, but I have to throw a bit of science in this and I will try to stay as basic as I can. You might even want to take a moment and allow some time to reflect what's I'm about to say next. All elements on the periodical chart are composed of the same basic components – protons, neutrons, and electrons. What makes one element different from the other is how energy is placed which gives rise to its numbers the dictate its structures.

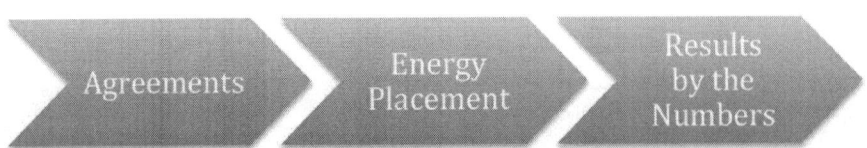

Then you have chemical compounds, which primarily extend out of how elements combine. So every last thing that you see in existence is resulting from numbered energy or how protons, neutrons and electrons are placed, and then combinations of energy. Everything in life is energy and not matter. Mostly, when you combine compounds, you then get more active and visible energy.

The physical body you live in is just a series of combined compounds, which is simply pure energy, all in a constant state of movement, but more importantly, a constant state of exchange.

Now, what is vital know here is that all energy is experienced based on how energy exchanges. You cannot have an experience without exchange. You yourself and all the energy associated with you are in a constant state of exchange. All exchanges are intimate in nature whether you recognize the exchange or not.

So, let's simplify all of this. You are in a constant state of getting pregnant and a constant state of birthing. When we think of pregnancy and giving birth, they are only thought of in general as an event stemming from a sexual union, but sex, sexuality, and a sexual union serves as a model of how the Universe works in its entirety. As a matter of fact, when you consider Universal Laws, the act of having sex, getting pregnant, and then delivering a newborn is elementary in comparison to how energy works on all dimensions of Universal existence.

The Universal Law of Everything

You are constantly having babies whether you realize it or not. Universally, whenever there is an exchange, it can only happen if there is some type of union for that exchange to happen. So intimacy happens on so many levels, it is very hard to comprehend. With this I can confidently say, because you are pure energy, you then are also in a constant state of intimacy. Yes, you are constantly connecting, more so, you are constantly getting pregnant and you are constantly producing.

This happens whether you are consciously participating or not. Even when bad things happen, you made that baby.

The Anatomy of Time

If I can continue to influence you to drop the concept of physicality and adopt the idea of experiencing life from an energy base, you can then acquire tools that will give you absolute control of how things turn out in your life, wipe out the notion of emptiness, and close your distances. Yes, you have absolute control. The problem of controlling the results in your life all stem from not having the knowledge of what needs to be controlled. Whether you have control or not, life will always exchange with life, otherwise life would cease to exist because all exchanges lead to results. With every exchange, there is a result.

How do you obtain the desired results you want consistently?

Do not just think of life or energy as that which expands out into infinity as the universe expands, but also think of life or energy the composition of life as that which enfolds in at the deepest levels of density. So infinity travels both ways, inside and out. But as it concerns life and its energy make-up, these exchanges have no meaning unless there is some type of control. Who does the controlling? You. Moreover, it is you and your corresponding agreements that constitute control, but most people are ignorant of their surrounding agreements. This is what needs to change. Whether you are aware or not, these corresponding agreements are making babies. It is only by recognizing what these agreements are and thusly controlling them that gives life its meaning and purpose.

You control your results by controlling your agreements.

Let me explain what I mean by control. Every building that you see is a controlled form of energy. Every last man-made object is a controlled form of energy, the food you buy and eat, the car you drive in, the house you live in, the furniture that you sleep and sit on, the appliances that you use, the cell phone you talk on, your computers and tablets you use to communicate, the cups you drink out of, the toilets you pee in, the airplanes you travel on, the money you spend etc. Everything is controlled energy. They all got there by being birthed in someone's mind. Even that birth which is portrayed as a thought is pure energy, but it becomes controlled energy as it relates to the next individual's ability to agree with that thought and then actively agree with that thought.

You will be surprised as to how many active unconscious disagreements you might have around you sitting within your personal atmosphere. When things aren't going as planned and then you can't figure out why, it is the energy of the matter. Point blank. Period. Wrong results are babies born out of connections that birth new energies whether it's intentional or unintentional, conscious or unconscious. Because you are energy, you are constantly making connections, and you are constantly in contact with other energies that always supply results. But a lot of people have become disassociated with this fact because of their understanding as to how life really works.

Everything you see and experience around you is a result. It did not get there without some type of relational agreement.

Let me do something here that's probably never been done before. I need to take a commercial break in this book to allow for a public service announcement. **COMMERCIAL BREAK:**

Many religions have done mankind a huge disservice by playing up the role of God and playing down the role of man. This is a form of escapism. A fleeing from responsibility, or better stated, a fleeing from a person's ability to respond. Why do I say this? Everything that we don't understand or can't make sense of, we throw it to the realm of spirituality where from the invisible, some being is making all this stuff happen. When things go bad, it's the devil. When things go well, it's the grace and mercy of God. Even within the modern religious ideology, when things go bad, it's still God teaching us great lessons.

Under this religious notion, our minds are never positioned to mature, because everything is psychologically pushed beyond our personal control into "God's hand", therefore we never address the systemic existence of relationships around us that we are having legitimate and illegitimate babies with. People blame legitimate and their illegitimate results on both God and/or the devil, which distracts them from the source of their real issues – who and what they are tied to.

Yes God exist. But you are made in His image. We can't let this fact disintegrate into a watered down, religious meaning of struggle and survival. The image of God never dissipates or diminishes, so the model for what we can do and accomplish can never be minimal, minimized, or set up for a redo by God. God is not working it out, He is not trying to fix it, He is not trying to save us, God is not fighting the devil on our behalf, God is not cleaning up behind our mistakes and messes. God is. And because He is, we are. We only chose not to be at times by slowing down the cycles of our guaranteed results when we connect with people who drag down our dreams. So people pray for an answer from God verses being smart about who they surround themselves with.

Yes all of your results are guaranteed.

NOW BACK TO OUR REGULAR PROGRAMMING:

Energy is and is not to be. Energy can only be experienced by how you and I chose to express it. Expression is birthed out of our connections, which then directs and redirect energy. So new forms of energy are birthed out of our connections all the time. New forms of energy are birthed out of how you and I decide to make our agreements, so here then, the word intimacy comes into play.

Intimacy and Timing

When I think of intimacy, I'm not necessarily talking about sexual intimacy. Here, I am talking about the power of engagement and the power of attention. This is the power of being involved and the power of knowing that somebody cares about what you want. This is the basis of true intimacy. Deep involvement. Nothing happens without agreement, but in addition to that, there are no results without action towards these agreements. That's why integrity is important, and intimacy should run close behind commitment.

1. Make sure your connections care about what you want.
2. Look for active attention from those same connections.

First of all, attention is vital. You cannot have people in your life that can't invest the proper level of attention needed for authentication. There are people that have a systemic existence of friends around them that are shallow and couldn't make a decision towards what you want to do, even if you paid them. These type of people need to be eliminated from your life. Intimacy is not only about the attention received, but the resulting actions based on that attention. This happens to women a lot. Men give the highest attention with verbal acclamations and proclamations. For some women, this becomes enough; he said it, and I feel good about it. So then their personal value is based off of words and not action. Intimacy is about words and actions.

Words plus Action equals Intimacy.

I have broken down intimacy further into four components. They are as follows:

1. Consciousness
2. Communication
3. Connection
4. Commitment

Consciousness is about attention. You cannot have unconscious people around you. Even a conversation with that type of person will be bad. These people will always be asking,

"What are you talking about?",
"What did you just say? I don't understand that."
"What did you just do? I don't get you."

So on and so on... Conversations with these people become very difficult and strained because they are unconscious of your drive towards your destiny. You can say let's go in one direction, they will say, no let us go in this direction. Not only will your conversation be strained, but all of your movements will be strained also. You need people that pay attention. You need people that offer good communication and understanding. You need people who know how to connect. You need people around you that know how to stay committed towards your optimal direction.

Lacking any of these things will eventually show up in the timing of your results. People will ask you, what is wrong with you? You might not even know. But I can tell you, it's the relationships that you build.

Remember, pay attention to the energies around you. There is always an exchange, impregnations, gestation periods, and births happening constantly. If you really understood the accuracy of this statement and then understood the gravity of this statement, you would immediately force yourself to be hyperconscious of who and what you have around you. There are people carrying your soon to be children and you are carrying within you other people's children. Children here are your ideas that are set in time to eventually become reality.

Now the "eventually" or the timing of your results are left completely up to you. Let me explain how this works by breaking down the anatomy of time. Time marks the evolution of ideas that eventually becomes a reality based on your connections. Ideas never determine what happens in time, your connections do. Once a connection happens, the clock starts. Time here is equivalent to the gestation period of a baby. The gestation period for a human baby is about nine months, and then the baby is primarily born within the tenth month. So the time ratio here is 9 then 1, which equals 10.

Everything that is considered to be a species on this planet from plants to animals has different gestation periods that lead to completion. In the same light you have different ideas and desires, and once planted, they each have their own gestation periods or cycles. At the end of it all, something is produced or birthed. Ideas never die, but the cycle or timing of ideas coming into reality for experience is varied. All ideas and desires are hinged on who you decide to impregnate with the idea or desire. Within the realm of energy, when it comes to birthing something that comes from the mind, gestation is based on who is receiving your idea and desire and then their level of passion towards what you want to accomplish, followed up by active agreement which is intimacy.

Some people cannot carry your babies, so stop getting them pregnant. A good bit of time you cannot accomplish what you want in life because you are pregnant with to much stuff that belongs to other people. Stay with me. This is a non-gender specific notion. You pick up live fetuses of other peoples crap and disasters just by hanging around them and exchanging energy with them. We have to stop being surprised by the crap that happens in our lives and begin notating the people, places, and things we associate with that's getting us pregnant. You might be hurting, but not by means of anything you have done. You're just pregnant with someone else pain or issues. Sex and intimate exchange is happening on more levels and dimensions than you might have been previously aware of.

Let me give you a couple of examples:

You can talk to certain people and then walk away with the energy of their issues. In the same light, you can converse or spend some time with others and leave you pregnant with new ideas, visions, and enthusiasm.

You can also walk into certain places and then when you leave, you leave with the energy of that place built inside you. Good or bad. In the same way the energy of things can become imbedded inside you. I always advise people to go through their house and work-spaces and get rid of broken things and unused items within their environment.

There are people when it comes to their personal relationships, they keep failing; a long string of break-ups, fights, separation and divorces. It never seems to work. What they might not realize is that they are pregnant with an end-result well before it becomes an end result. It could be as simple as the TV shows they are watching. If they watch shows like the daytime soaps where there is constant relationship failures, they are actually walking away from the television pregnant with those failed relationship models. People can get pregnant from the neighborhood they live in, the energy of the school they might attend, or even the energy of the church they attend.

COMMERCIAL BREAK AGAIN:

In most African American churches people are taught this about God, "That He may not get there when you want Him, but He is always there on time". What a dangerous and horrible spiritual concept. This leaves many people with the notion that life is about there being a "devil" that is abusing them, and then God will soon rescue them at his leisure. The Christian Bible actually teaches that God is always with you, better yet, being made in God's image leaves you with full God capabilities of manifestation and accomplishment. Yet they say stupid stuff like, "God sits up high and looks down low"...

I was never the one who could fully enjoy a good superhero movie or TV show. Back in my day there was Batman and Robin, Superman, Spiderman, Ultraman, Voltron, Shazam and the like. They were all based on the same premise. The "evil" enemy would abuse and terrorize the city and even the superhero at times, as his or her "regular" self would be also be abused and terrorized. BUT WAIT! Towards the end the show or the movie superman would go into the phone booth, batman would go to his bat cave, Ultraman would pull out his light wand and push the button and so on. Then they would change into the superhero! Then as the superhero, they would then proceed to annihilate the evil enemy. But what would be upsetting to me is why could they not have saved themselves and everybody else from the beginning of the movie or the TV show by starting off as the superhero? Dahhhh...

What???!!!?

If that happened, you wouldn't have the drama needed to cover a half hour show or a 2-hour movie. The show would be over before it began if they used their superpowers early on. So it is primarily in the African American church. A "Divine Drama" is preached every Sunday about all the struggles you have to suffer while you wait on God to suit up to come and save the day. So God is treated as a superhero while one is taught to suffer in the mean time. Watch this. Now being pregnant with this Drama, people go home and live it out in their life outside the church.

The energy dynamic of the church's "God and the devil" drama is implanted within the person's spirit and they birth out the same paralleling drama over time within other instances of within their life.

Get the picture. It's all just energy. Whether it's something you believe in or don't believe in, something you hold sacred, a religious ideology, or one person says this, the other person says that, it could be a cause, or it can be a movement, it's all just energy. You can go to church week after week and listen to every word, and it could have nothing to do with what you want in life; but if that's your association, you will get pregnant with something that leads you away or distract you from your destiny.

Nobody wants to ask the tough questions. People just repeat the same behaviors over and over again. You have to set your desire, set your wants, and set forth your ideas then ask the following tough questions:

1. Is what I am doing have anything to do with what I want? If it is no, stop it! No matter how holy someone says that it is.
2. What are we? Is the person or persons I associate with and the exchanges within those associations mirror my destiny or desire? If not, drop it!

Here, I used an example of church and how some view God. But this can be applied to anything or any belief system. You are designed to accomplish life and then obtain the life you want, anything else is following somebody else's ideals and having their dead-end babies.

BACK TO THE SHOW:

Lastly, you can get pregnant from the energies of people. Plain and simple. You must launch an awareness campaign and pay acute attention to your personal environment of personages.

Every relationship you have provides an energy dynamic. This dynamic in turn becomes an entity much like sperm that is implanted and fertilized. You never know what a person you associate with is carrying and what energy dynamics you might be taking on from them. Every conversation, every interaction, every exchange provides a basis for pregnancy, gestation, and then results.

If you are looking for results, these results always come in time over a gestation period. Then there is a manifestation and birthing of the results. So going back to what needs to be controlled is as follows, you must control your:

1. Control what you think about. Be specific about your wants and desires.
2. Control your energy environment, which leads to your personal intimate exchanges. Your environment must relate to your wants and desires. This includes people, places, and things.
3. Measurement of your exchanges give you control over your gestation times and cycles.

The timing and the reveal of your results you want are tied up in who is pregnant around you due to their intent intimacy towards your dream. The better you chose and make arrangements here, the more efficient your timing, cycles, and gestation periods are.

You control it. You must take responsibility for your future. A good strategy involves what I call the law of accounting.

The Strategies for Significance

I want to give you the Structure of Significance, and if you follow and commit to the structure, you will find yourself significantly empowered to do and accomplish whatever you want in life.

First I will start by giving you the unknown Law Of Accounting, which is the Anatomy Of Significance. Trust me, this law becomes the core of all of the other laws of existence. In actuality, this law is very easy to understand and to comprehend, but it is also so simple that it can be easily misunderstood or not understood at all. So try to not to do too much thinking and I promise you, you will gain a sense of freedom and empowerment that you might not have previously experienced or felt before. The following are the components of the Law of Accounting:

1. Mind Body
2. Emotional Body
3. Relationship Accounts Body
4. Time Body (Outer Mirror)
5. Inner Mirror (Your Spirit)
6. Energy Body
7. Universal Response Body
8. Your Completions Body

After this, I will introduce to you a new system of recognizing intelligence, The 8 Intelligence Strata. In these intelligence strata you will find eight levels of intelligence in which you can identify your current place of awareness and operation as well as others. This intelligence stratus will provide you with the bases of how you engage people and how people should engage you. Here are the 8 Intelligence Strata:

1. Primal
2. Basic
3. Advanced
4. Coordinal
5. Creative
6. Innovative
7. Clairvoyant Constructive
8. All Knowing

Then I will provide you with 4 Points of Measurements in order to count out the responses invested within yourself by others. One of the things that people do not do within their relationships is to take measurements. If you do not take measurements, you will be taken. Taken for granted. Even when you walk into a store, a system of measurements is set that determines the exchange when you walk out with products or services. If that did not exist, the value of what people get as they shop will be taken for granted. So everything that is in the store is measured, or more correctly, priced before you engage with that product or service. You must set your personal price in order to have optimal relationship experiences. Here are the 4 Points of Measurement:

1. Measured Motifs   The 1st Relationship Set
2. Measured Money   The 2nd Relationship Set
3. Measure Moments   The 3rd Relationship Set
4. Measured Monuments   The 4th Relationship Set

Once you lock in these, I will then give you what I call The 12 Points Of Significance. These points are designed to help you further measure your exchanges with others. The need for this is vital. When you experience a diminished ability or capability to gain what you want in life, it is usually due to what you're actually receiving in life from others. This too must be measured and quantified if you plan to live successfully.

Once you finish out of these, I fully expect you to be a master at relationships and a master within the exchanges you make in life. This mastery should immediately be reflected into all other areas of your life including your health, your wealth, and then your ability and capability to gain anything that comes to your mind. Here are the 12 Points of Significance:

1. To Be Viewed
2. To Be Comprehended
3. To Be Engaged
4. To Be Praised
5. To Be Believed
6. To Be Prioritized
7. To Be Enriched

8. To Be Advanced
9. To Be Rewarded
10. To Be Exalted
11. To Be Increased
12. To Be Doubled or Mirrored

All of these strategies can be used to gain a greater since of significance. It would be good to put some of these points and structures to memory so they can become a part of your deeper conscious.

The Gift of Pushing

As mentioned earlier, from the earliest points of earth's history, even including the earliest points of the Universe, life pushed from one level to the next. But in order for the next to happen, energy had to be present. Now that we know that energy is a product of relationship, we can now take a worldview that to mature to the next level, relationship played and currently plays a vital role in growth. This is embedded into all of creation and has occurred naturally for millions of years. As life pushed to new levels, everything in existence was codependent on something else. Life generated new life. Like-kind birthed out like-kind, and everything remained interrelated.

But recently in Earth's history humankind made a shift in consciousness about 10,000 years ago. Civilizations began to appear as proven by archeological finds worldwide. Humankind had shifted from a primal existence to a level of conscious awareness that began a new kind of push. Although mankind in its primitive states before this advanced stage, man had already began to form tribal and family units, but self-awareness did not exist nor did an advanced awareness of the other existed. The environment controlled the mind and developmental direction. Survival was the order of the day.

Then reaching this new level of existence 10,000 years ago, a new type of pushing in nature now existed. Instead of the environment pushing advancement, now the human mind was capable of pushing advancement. But something was real new here, but still nestled within the primal with all the potential to grow. This new thing was the ability to choose and select relationships based on creation and advancement. Humankind was no longer subject to the environment and the mind could now look over and above the environment and create its own environments for comfort, but forming these new corresponding relationships at this stage was still primitive. Humankind had to choose relationships that supported these funny new dreams of creating something new, organizing things for more efficient use, and seeing great new possibilities through the process of discovery and research.

The human body was flooding with advanced chemicals called the emotions that helped humankind to map out corresponding relationships to his or her dreams and desires. A goal would be set, the body would agree, but now one needed support from others to reach their goals. For the first time insignificance kicked in because the next person, the next mind could choose to be something different. Loneliness kicked in. It is not good for man to be alone. Man would now grow societies with common goals and ideals. Some civilizations thrived. Some came and quickly died out. Within all of this, something new existed that would mirror how nature had performed millions of years earlier. Pushing. Creative pushing. Innovative pushing.

Here is the point. From the earliest days of modern civilization, a person would come up with an advancement. Of course, this advancement only existed within his or her mind. In order for this thought to become reality a person must begin to express his ideas to others, but nothing could or would happen unless the one hearing the expressed idea or desire decided to push the idea with his or her own skill set. So now enters into human history the need for agreement, like mindedness, and significance. The ability to push another into their greatness is a gift. To be pushed into your greatness in the point of significance.

The Law of Accounting

Chapter 2

The Law of Accounting

I'm going to show you little known secret called the Law of Accounting. It's really not about what you count in the end, but it's about taking account of what you relate to in the beginning. The Law Of Accounting consists of 8 components. These components are the totality of who you are in the world. They are as follows:

1. Mind Body
2. Emotional Body
3. Relationship Accounts Body
4. Time Body (Outer Mirror)
5. Inner Mirror (Your Spirit)
6. Energy Body
7. Universal Response Body
8. Your Completions Body

These eight bodies are the construct of your entire body system. They are all intimately interrelated. One does not function without the other. Just as your natural body is a complete system of relationships, these eight bodies are a complete system of relationships that govern your existence. It is the balance of these eight bodies that gives you significance. The key here is having an awareness that these eight bodies exists and are at work at all times.

I will chart out these eight items in the hopes of giving you a clear understanding as to how they work. The chart looks as follows:

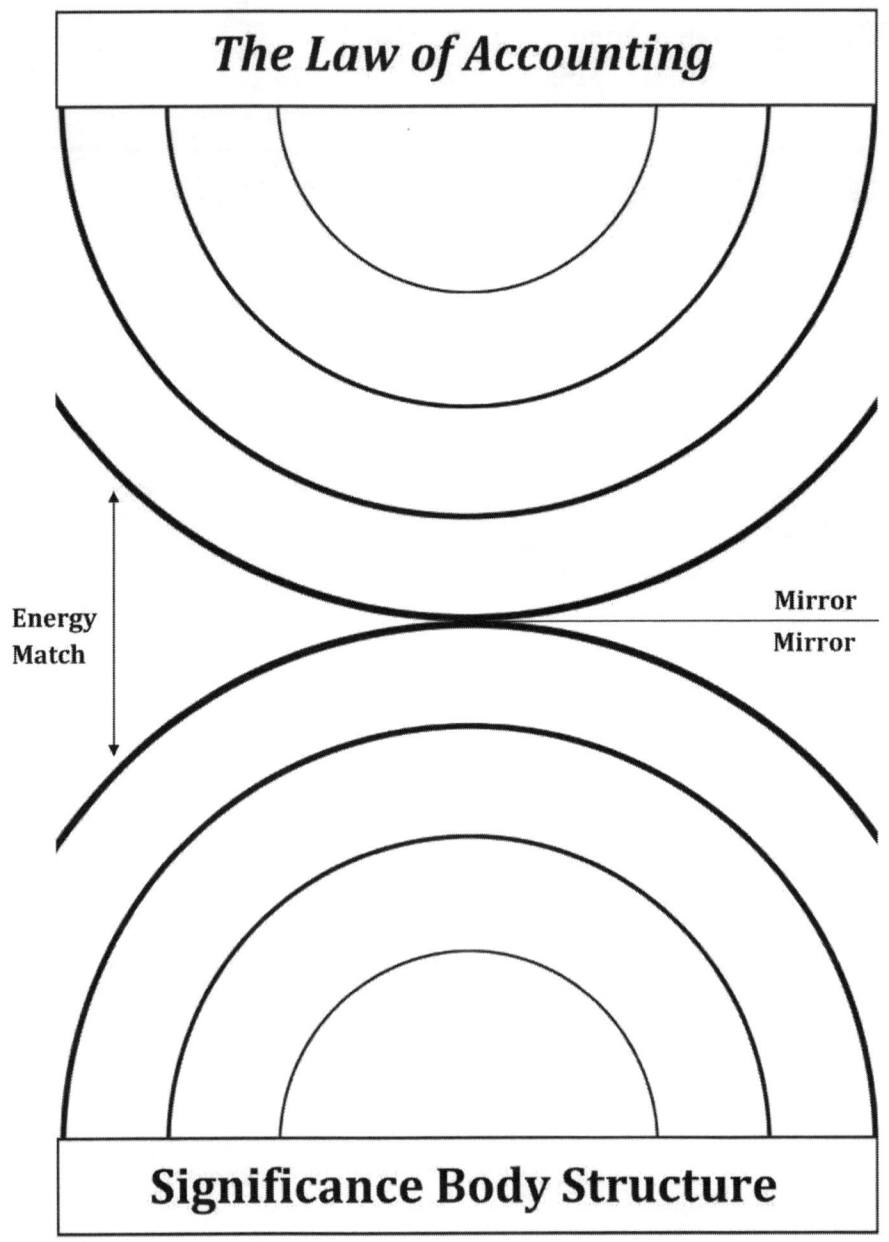

There are four cycles at the top and then there are four cycles at the bottom. The four cycles at the top mirror the four cycles at the bottom. Another key to notice here is that the energy of the top cycles will always match the energy of the bottom cycles. To restate this, there are a total of eight cycles divided in half with the top four mirroring the bottom four. Please get this in your head, because as we fill out the chart, you'll get an easy understanding of all the relationships within and therefore you will be able to use this law to maintain a great sense of significance at all times.

1. Four Cycles At The Top
2. Four Cycles At The Bottom
3. The Top Mirrors The Bottom
4. Both The Top And Bottom Carry The Same Energy

So let's look at the first component of the Law of Accounting, the Mind Body.

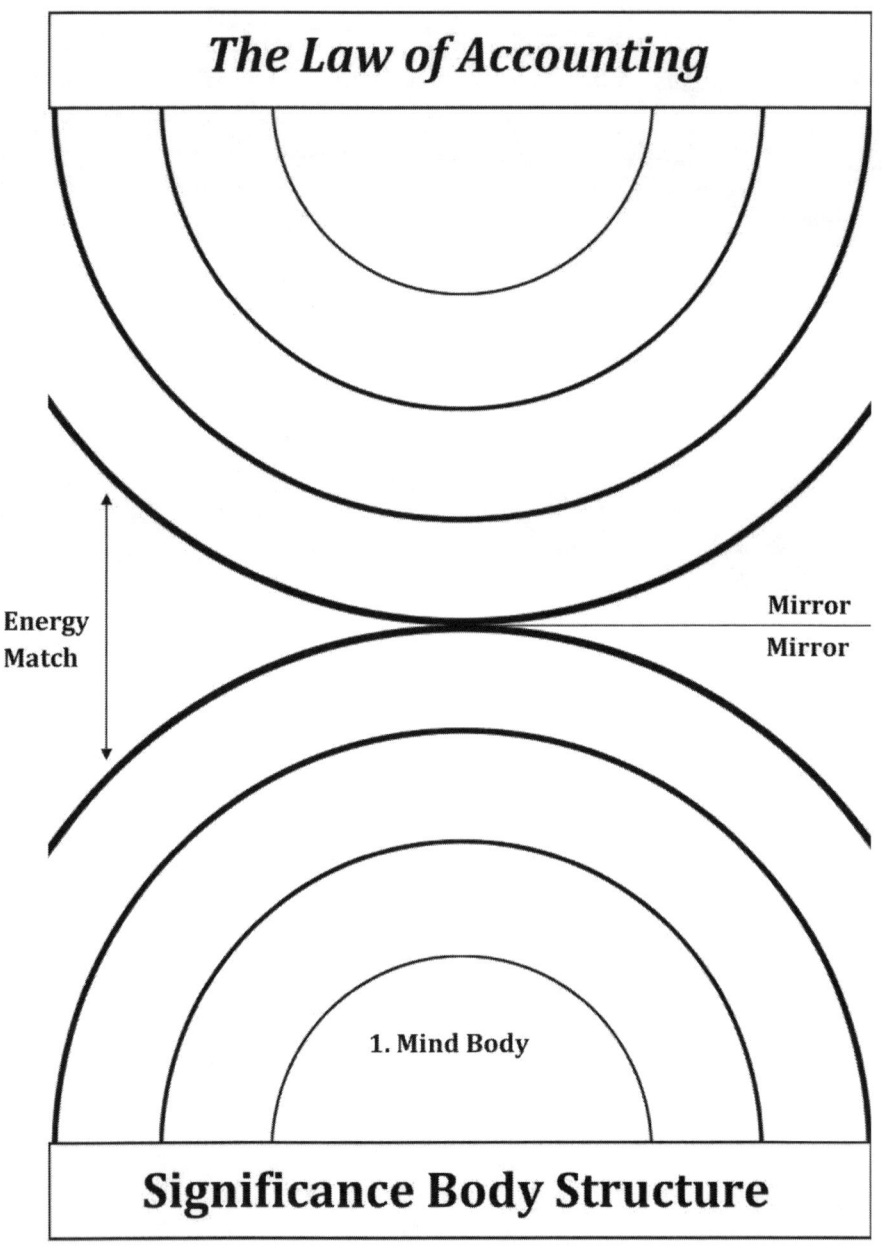

The Mind Body

The mind is anything that exists outside of what we might consider to be physical or compressed energy. The body represents compressed energy. The mind is still the body because the physical body only represents the same energy of the mind but on a denser level. What you see when you look at the body is only a container representing or mirroring what can't be seen. It is through this container, the body, that we experience what is to be experienced. The compressed visible container is only an extension of the invisible, which is the Mind Body.

To better understand what I mean by container, you can view the body as the storage unit for the mind. This is what we call memory. The brain is not the only container for memory, but your whole body contains memory. The whole body works as a computer disk drive for the mind. But the mind itself is nothing more than a transfer station for your thoughts. Let me explain.

Nothing happens in life until you form a relationship to what has happened in order for it to exist as something that has happened. Like a tree falling down in a forest, the tree has not fallen to you until you via some way of communication with the facts of the tree falling has the tree actually fallen. But you must determine in your mind that that is the definition of that event. As soon as you set this definition in your mind that the tree has fallen, it transfers via the neurons in the brain, in which the neurons, which are only a combination of water and electricity, mirror the definition of that event which is determined by you. Then and only then is the fact of the tree falling become processed, stored within the body, and deemed a reality. This storage of information in the body then and only then becomes a presence to you and a reality.

A bit much to swallow, huh?

So let's ask this question? When does something happen? An event may take place that you may witness, but the event hasn't actually happened yet. You have to go into nanoseconds to fully process the importance of this. I'll ask the question again. When does something happen?

Here is a fact. Things cannot have happened without your mind processing it as being so. When an event takes place, your five senses will soon pick up on that event, but it still takes time for that event to travel from its origin or source of activity to eventually meet your eyes, ears, nose, mouth, or skin for processing by your mind. Even though it seems instantaneous to you, there is still a nanosecond of time that passes before an event or action reaches you. Makes sense?

It is this "time" in between the event's origin and then the mental processing of the event that becomes vital to the mind and it's functioning. Between the time an event leaves its source or origin of activity and then reaches your mind, to you, within that time that event has not happened yet. As the event begins to hit your sensorium, the event still has not happened yet until you make some determinations as to what it is that has happened. It is within these split nanoseconds that ten people can technically witness the same event, but all ten persons can walk away with ten different experiences. You can interview each one and ask them, "What happened?", and you can get ten different answers all stemming from the same event. Next question.

Is what "happened" the event that took place at its source or origin, or is it what happened the same event as it is processed by the ten different minds? The answer.

Happenings are not happenings until it is processed by you. So here is one event mirrored in ten different minds as ten different events or experiences. An event can't be what it is without you giving it its definition. So I'll restate it this way, it is the relationship that you build as you exchange with an event that causes the event to become a "happening". Why is this important?

Reality does not happen to you, reality starts with you. It is within this time, the time between the origins of an event and when the event happens as it processed by you, where all power exists. Remember, it is all energy. You and I always have the power to determine these energy mixes as things happen. It is the determination of these energy-mixes that form the basis of creation, reality and experience.

Reality does not happen to you, reality starts with you.

The mind-brain relationship is fascinating. Based on how you process an event, an electrical line of energy is formed and emitted in the brain, and water travels along this electrical impulse to form what is called a neuron. This neuron is the first component of memory. This neuron is actually new life. What you would really need to know here is this; an event is only a fleeting moment and cannot remain in reality; it comes and then it goes, but the neuron formed in the brain becomes the first component of reality that will remain with you forever. Reality exists based only on how you process an event and thusly how this electricity and water responds. This response is new life. This is so vital, you must read this paragraph again and again until you get it.

Your local presence is the only reality that exists.

Ok. Here's where I get to mess with your mind. An event within itself can never be a reality because it actually comes and goes. Only how you process an event is reality, meaning, the only reality in existence is you. I'm sure the bottom just dropped out of some of your brains, but read it again.

An event within itself can never be a reality because it actually comes and goes, only how you process an event is reality, meaning, the only reality in existence is within you. Life is a series of creations and these creations only arise out of how you process what you see, hear, taste, touch and smell, then store.

Life is not a series of events, nor is it "physical" existence. Life can only be what you decide to process and remember. Life is memory. Life can only be memory. There is no such thing as reality outside of what you decide to remember. Now, can you understand to vitalness of the mind and memory? It is the only entity that can be life. Please process this. It is your life that we are talking about here.

Let get to you this way. Remember, we talked about infinite density. As scientist, both chemist and biologist, as they probe deeper into "physical" matter, they are continuing to find that there is actually nothing there. The deeper they go, the more "nothing" that they find. It's all energy. So in reality, how you put things together in your mind is also just energy. You have the movement of energy and then you have how energy is processed in the mind and stored. That's it. Life. Movement and storage. Movement and comprehension.

Comprehension is the totality of life. You chose your level of comprehension. You choose your level of intelligence. You choose the level of how you exist within pure energy, which then constitutes life. With comprehension being the totality of what's comprehended, how are you comprehended by those you consider to be close to you?

So let's prove it with the simple example of the tree falling in the forest. I'm going to expand on this now.

The Anatomy of Memory

The tree has fallen in the forest. The tree has fallen in the forest across a road, blocking the road. The tree has fallen in the forest, blocking the road, but has landed on a car. The tree has fallen in the forest, blocking the road, but has landed on a car with a family in it. The tree has fallen in the forest, blocking the road, but has landed on a car with a family in it, and the family was hurt. The tree has fallen in the forest, blocking the road, but has landed on a car with a family in it, and the family was hurt, and there were emergency vehicles everywhere. The tree has fallen in the forest, blocking the road, but has landed on a car with a family in it, and the family was hurt, and there were emergency vehicles everywhere while it was pouring down rain.

Several people witnessed this event. The local news station was on the scene interviewing several witnesses asking people, "What happened?". Here are their answers:

Witness #1, a forester said, a tree fell.
Witness #2, a busy businessman said, the road was blocked and I was late for work.
Witness #3, a curious child said, I saw a whole bunch of lights flashing.
Witness #4, a concerned citizen said, a whole family was injured in an accident.
Witness #5, a clueless bystander said, I was stuck in the rain.
Witness #6, a driver in the next car said, a tree just missed

	hitting my car.
Witness #7,	a car enthusiast said, a Mercedes Benz was crushed by a tree, Oh my God.
Witness #8,	a doctor said, there were multiple contusions and lacerations, but the family is ok.
Witness #9,	a nervous person said, I saw the accident, my heart stopped, I started sweating etc.
Witness #10,	an aspiring actress said, look Ma, I'm on TV.

There is one event, 10 different takeaways. What happened? What is reality?

Life is a response to how and what you process in the mind that then becomes memory, starting with the formation of an electrical impulse and water called neurons. Now in addition, there are chemicals in your body that respond to the construct of these neurons in the brain, and your body itself becomes a responsive enforced memory that mirrors the neurons. Scientist calls these chemicals, emotions. Your body is a composition of chemical movements and secretions. Creation doubles that quickly through the brain via the neurons and then the body chemically as you process events within the mind. This all happens within nanoseconds.

Every event that is witnessed by you can be processed to benefit you.

This is the first construct of the mind. This is the mind as it responds to events. This is the mind as it responds to the environment. Your first point of control in all of this is what's done in that nanosecond of time between an event and then the impact of that event upon your senses. It is here that you must train your mind how to process events so that every event is processed to benefit you. Yes, every event that is witnessed by you can be processed to benefit you. Meaning, good or bad, negative or positive, no matter the type event, you can create new neurons based on how you decide to take in and process events. Remember, the event is not the reality; the processing of the event is the reality. Life is what you decide to carry as memory.

Deciding What You Want, Is the Best Memory

The second construct of the mind involves your desire. By having definite desires, it becomes the tool that affects the first construct of the mind. Believe it or not, it is by having desires and definite chosen direction that impacts how you process all other events. So the creation of your dream determines how all events impact you. This intentional focus forces new neuron creations to be in line with where you are going.

There are people who are acutely affected by things that happen around them. Their environment acutely affects them. What's outside them rules them. The question is why? First, they must realize that to be in such a position is primitive and primal. It's an old mind activity of the primitive man and animals. A person must mature from the effects of this type of mind activity. What changes this environmental responsive position is assigning to the mind a vision, a desire, and a destination. When this happens, you build neurons that are not environmentally activated or determined by the processing of events. Here, you build new memory outside of any events, circumstances, situations, or environmental concerns. This same special memory, memories of something that hasn't even happened yet, is a very special function of the mind.

Having a set desire, destiny, or direction affects the health of the mind. Desire and direction helps you to disassociate with the chemicals that are built in the body as a result of the environment that is directly mirrored from the neurons.

Now if you accept the fact that life is only the memory you hold, and life can't be the events or anything you witness with your five senses, then it can only remain a fact that the neurons created by your vision of the future your desire is also life. You cannot only assign memory to past events. This is where we rob ourselves. When you create neurons that stem from your future dreams and desires, they are still yet neurons. Yes. Not only are you left to process events that immediately drop of into past existence, but you also can do a different type of processing. You can process something new that never existed before, and this process of creating desires creates neurons, which is still life. It is still energy.

Watch this. One might say, the future, well it hasn't happened yet so it doesn't exist. Well neither does any event that just happened, it doesn't exist anymore as it falls into the past, but yet it is a part of your memory. It is your memory that forces existence. It is your memory that constitutes existence. It is your memory that constitutes life. Memory is life. So in contrast, in believing non-existence in terms of events and the environment, when you create new memory, this new memory actually exists. The power of your future and reality is just as strong as the power of your past and reality.

The reality of a future event exists just as much as the reality of a past event.

The reality of a future event exists just as much as the reality of a past event. What makes a future event hard to grasp for some, is the level of support and agreement from others that helps to authenticate the future that helps to authenticate your desires, and that helps to authenticate your dream. But the future, when thought of, always posits its reality immediately. The experience of a future reality, no matter how grand, comes into existence as soon as the neurons are formed. To better understand this I will need you to see the chart from the bottom up.

8. Your Completions Body
7. Universal Response Body
6. Energy Body
5. Inner Mirror
4. Time Body
3. Relationships Accounts Body
2. Emotional Body
1. Mind Body

Now let's input some thoughts and a few elements that's needed to digest this paradigm:

1. Desire – Your Uniqueness
2. Attention – Your Points of Focus
3. Perspective – What You Choose To See

The Law of Accounting

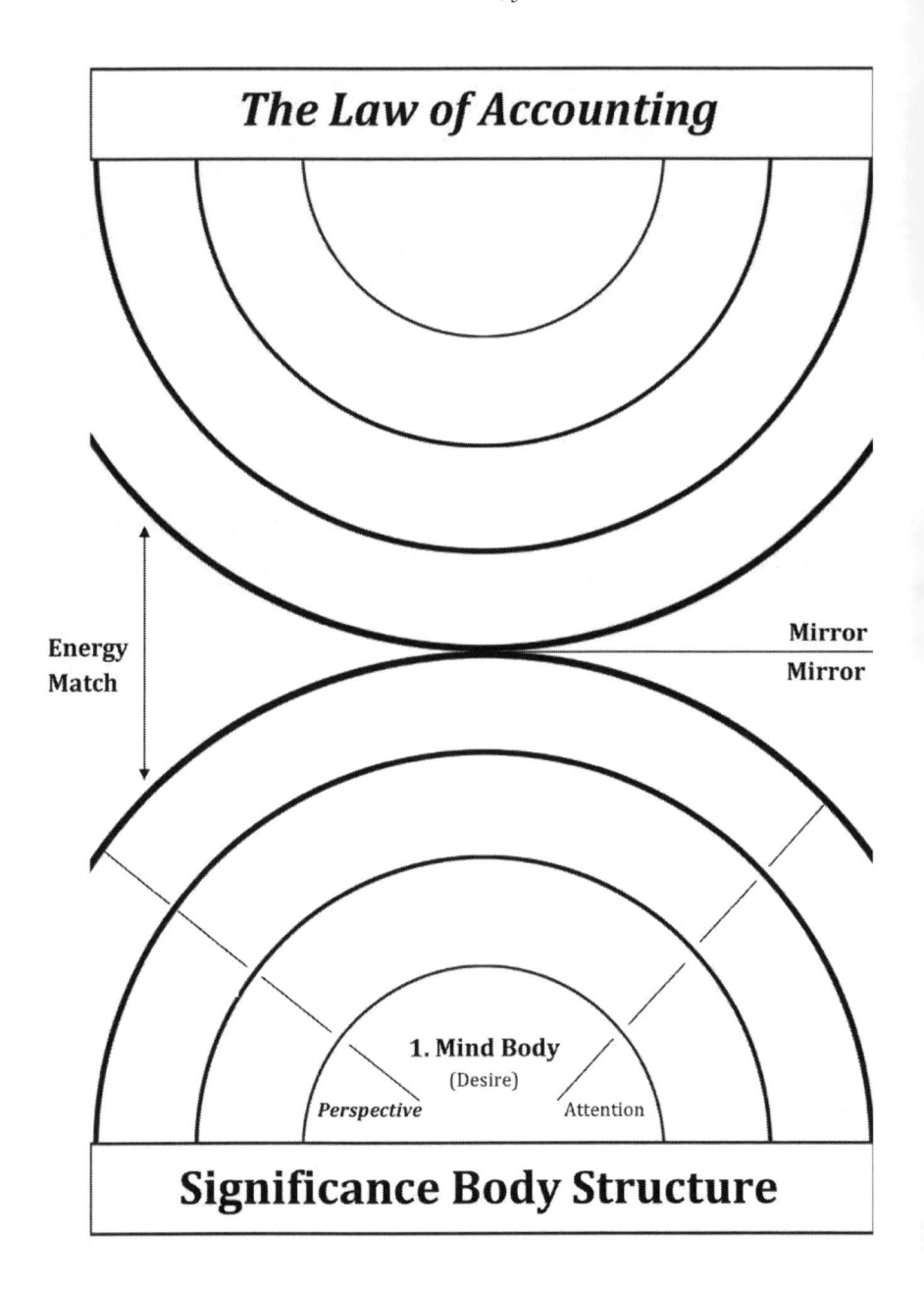

Mirror
Mirror

Energy Match

1. Mind Body
(Desire)
Perspective   Attention

Significance Body Structure

Desire

For a good number of people and for the most part, a high value is not placed on things. Every "thing" started from what could not be seen as an idea. It is Intelligence that possesses the ability to have an idea. You possess the ability to have an idea. Without ideas it is impossible to produce things. As I stated earlier, the very beginning of our Universe started with a thought, and that very thought had to be in the form of an idea.

Ideas start in the invisible. Any "thing" that exists in what cannot be seen is spirit. Your thoughts are spirit. Therefore, any "thing" that exists in the unseen is spiritual. Spirit starts in the unseen and makes its way to what can be seen. So my definition of anything that is spiritual is anything that is capable of moving from the unseen to what can be seen. This is the process of creation. To create is spiritual. To make something happen is spiritual. To produce is spiritual. To make things and to have things is spiritual. It has less to do with any religion, religious practice, or moving yourself into the spiritual by denying things, and more to do with being able to see in the spirit and creating into the physical those same things which are envisioned. Or might I say, InVision.

You are the substance of things hoped for, and you are the evidence of things not seen. True insight forces foresight. To create, to make something happen, and to produce is spiritual. The totality of existence exists within you. Your job is to bring the invisible existence into visible existence. Your job is to take vapor and make water, then freeze the water to make ice. None of this can happen without you having a dream, a desire, or some type of direction.

True insight forces foresight.

The whole purpose of Universal Intelligence, the whole reason for God is not to remain unseen and invisible. The process of being is based on what is mirrored into physical existence from what exist in the spirit, hence, what exist in the mind. This makes what you think highly valuable. There is an innate human need to mirror thought, and things are thoughts reflected into tangible reality. People who have few good things generally have few good thoughts. If this became common knowledge, people would pay more attention to the quality of their thoughts.

The concept of desire has a purpose. Desire is usually based on moving from one state of existence to better state of existence. This can be born out of being dissatisfied with your current state and the need to make things better. I can't express this enough, life is desire. Life is the ability to grow your desire, and growing is moving what's inside you to the outside.

Attention

Attention forces relevance or irrelevance.

You must pay attention to the quality of your thoughts, because you are designed in such a way that the Universe goes to immediate work to produce what's on your mind. That's why I tell people, "Do not dismiss your desires". What you desire in life is critical. It may be a new house, a new car, owning your own business so you can make millions or even billions, to have better relationships, or just to improve the overall quality of life. You can have all of these things based on what you decide to do with your desires and the attention you give them. If you dismiss your desires based on a low quality of thinking, you immediately dismiss the possibility of having those things.

The First Attention

The first attention happens in the unseen world of thought. It is "getting" you. It is self-awareness. You must catalog your desires and come up with the clear definitions of who you are. It is your personal perception. These are also your points of affirmation. And you must reaffirm yourself daily! You must have clear affirmations to know what the confirmations towards you have to be. So here, you must give heightened attention to your thought processes by building a portfolio of your mental assets before they hit your personal stock exchange. Remember, all energy is in a content state of exchange. How you focus and what you pay attention to determine your personal energy exchange. How you exchange plays a major role in self-value and significance.

The Second Attention

The second attention happens in the seen world of existences. It is how you relate to the things and people around you. It is the awareness of what matches your desires. You must design your physical surroundings to flow with what's in your head and terminate anything and anyone who doesn't get it. It is accepting your personal provisions. These are also your points of confirmation. And you must have the things and the people in your life to confirm you daily! These confirmations towards you must be clear and accurate and not left in the realm of potential and the hopeful. So here you must give heightened attention to this initial personal stock exchange so that your personal returns from others have value and significance.

Perspective - Choosing Your Line of Site

Remember the time that we talked about that exists between the source of an event and then the processing of the event by you. Here is where perspective plays a major role in your reactions to the environment and outside events. You must shape your perspective beforehand. Perspective is what you choose to see, it is choosing your line of site. Even though your mind processes over 400 million events per second, you still don't have time to think about how you are going process certain things or react to certain things.

The trick is, is to choose your reactions beforehand. This is the most powerful notion imaginable. First, is having the ability to choose. Second, is using a strategy of choosing beforehand. When a basketball player shoots a free throw, he is not choosing to make that free throw at that moment. There is so much pressure. Fans of the other team, all 15,000 plus are throwing every distraction imaginable. The lights are bright. The body is tired. Sweat is making the ball slippery. Even the music of the opposing team changes to dark music. Millions of variables are in place to move the mind away from making the shot. Yet the basketball player shoots with poise and ease and makes the free throw.

Always choose your reactions beforehand.

This is because he chose beforehand to make the shot and practiced many hours at making that shot until that shot became a memory. Many basketball games are won because the true basketball stars won the game beforehand by creating a memory of winning.

You have to train the mind to see what you want to see well before events happen. It's your training that shapes the event. Think about the time we don't spend training ourselves to be winners. You are designed to win, but you are responsible for creating the memory for winning. It is this memory that counteracts events that are not necessarily in your favor. More so, it is this memory that can pull elements out of unfavorable conditions and events and turn them into your favor.

Winning takes training.

Notice how when a basketball player's shoots a free throw in an opposing teams arena. Notice no matter how much noise and raucous is going on, when that player hits the free throw, the whole arena goes quite. It's like, "In your face!". One made shot by the player, shuts up 15,000 to 18,000 screaming fans at once. The energy of this simple shutdown saps the energy out of the opposing team. Shots like this become vital near the end of a game and the score is close. So the screaming fans and then the silencing of the fans become a tool and works towards the free throw shooter's advantage.

When you train your line of site, your line of site becomes dominant no matter what happens around you. Distractions are diminished. Other options are not entertained. Direction becomes steadfast. Conditions are ignored. All energy is consistently pulled in your direction. The non-optimal becomes optimal. The naysayers become silenced. The horrible becomes bearable.

Again, perspective is not set based on the environment or an event. Perspective is set in the mind by design, then training within that design. At the advent of portable electronic book readers, many bookstores that sold physical books went out of business. Only a couple of major book chains survived. It was the CEO's perspective of the market and industry that was set well in advance before the electronic book readers threatened the entire bookstore industry. As many other bookstores met this challenge as a tragedy, one bookstore met the same event and saw it as an opportunity. They then produced their own book reader and became its own competition. Brilliant!

What is your perspective? What do you choose to see in life? Do you allow people to influence what you see by their own understanding? Do you allow your surrounding environment, your circumstances, or events influence what you see? The entirety of your energy follows the direction of your line of site. To keep events or outside circumstances from influencing your direction, your mind must be trained beforehand. A racecar driver driving nearly 200 miles per hour into a curve is told; in order to keep from crashing into the wall, you must not look at the wall; you must look at the curve. Looking at the wall in an attempt to keep from crashing into the wall will pull you right into the wall.

You can never plan to win; you must remember to win.

This is well beyond the practice of visualization as taught by some personal development specialists. With the fact of what you desire, once desired, coming into immediate existence, it no longer needs to be visualized for manifestation. The process here is a bit different. Once you set a desire, the neurons create the fullness of that desire via electricity and water. Remember, this is all energy. The energy within you does the work of connecting with the like energy outside of you that's relative to your desire. Again, with this, the entirety of your desire comes into immediate existence.

Let me help you with this. Here's a small note on what is called sympathetic resonance. The neuron is a pocket of energy formed from water, h2o and electricity. This combination is a form of frequency. Frequency, once set, causes all similar frequencies within an environment to activate and vibrate. This happens within music all the time. Do not underestimate the power of this process. When you think, a thought, a great deal more is happening and is activated beyond your local thought.

So when you create a desire, an entire energy pool of your desire exists immediately, both within you and outside of you.

Now, the question is, what are your movements within this energy? It's not visualization that puts you at an advantage, but it is your line of site that then influences your movement. Perspective. With the energy of your desire existing in its entirety, this energy causes constant presentations of the necessary components of your dream towards you. People miss these presentations when their attention and line of site is misdirected. Their expectations are varied away from their own initiating thoughts.

1. Choose your reactions before hand by practicing your win. Create memory of winning.
2. It is your training that shapes future events.
3. Maintain a line of site to what already exists versus practicing visualization techniques. This is the practice of expectation.
4. Lock into what's tuned into you.

This is why I believe more in the Law of Supply versus the Law of Attraction. If something exists in its entirety, then you are not attracting it, nor are you attracting the components of it. But if what you want is fully supplied for because of frequency resonance, then it becomes a matter of waking up to what's in front of you and keeping it in your line of site. You then live with the expectancy of continuously running into and engaging what's for you that is consistent with your direction and desire.

Your Completions Body

The second component of Law of Accounting involves your completions although your completions are the 8th part within the Law Accounting. The reason that I'm skipping directly to the last component of the Law of Accounting is because the 1st and the 8th component come into existence simultaneously. This is actually a universal law and is generally not part of our awareness. Where this notion slips away is how we deal with time. We might think that we experience "time" between formulating an idea or a desire, and then the manifestation of the same. But this is far from the truth. You must give credence to the life of your ideas as they exist the moment you process the ideas in our mind.

So let's fill the next part the chart this way where the 1st mirrors the 8th.

What Is Life?

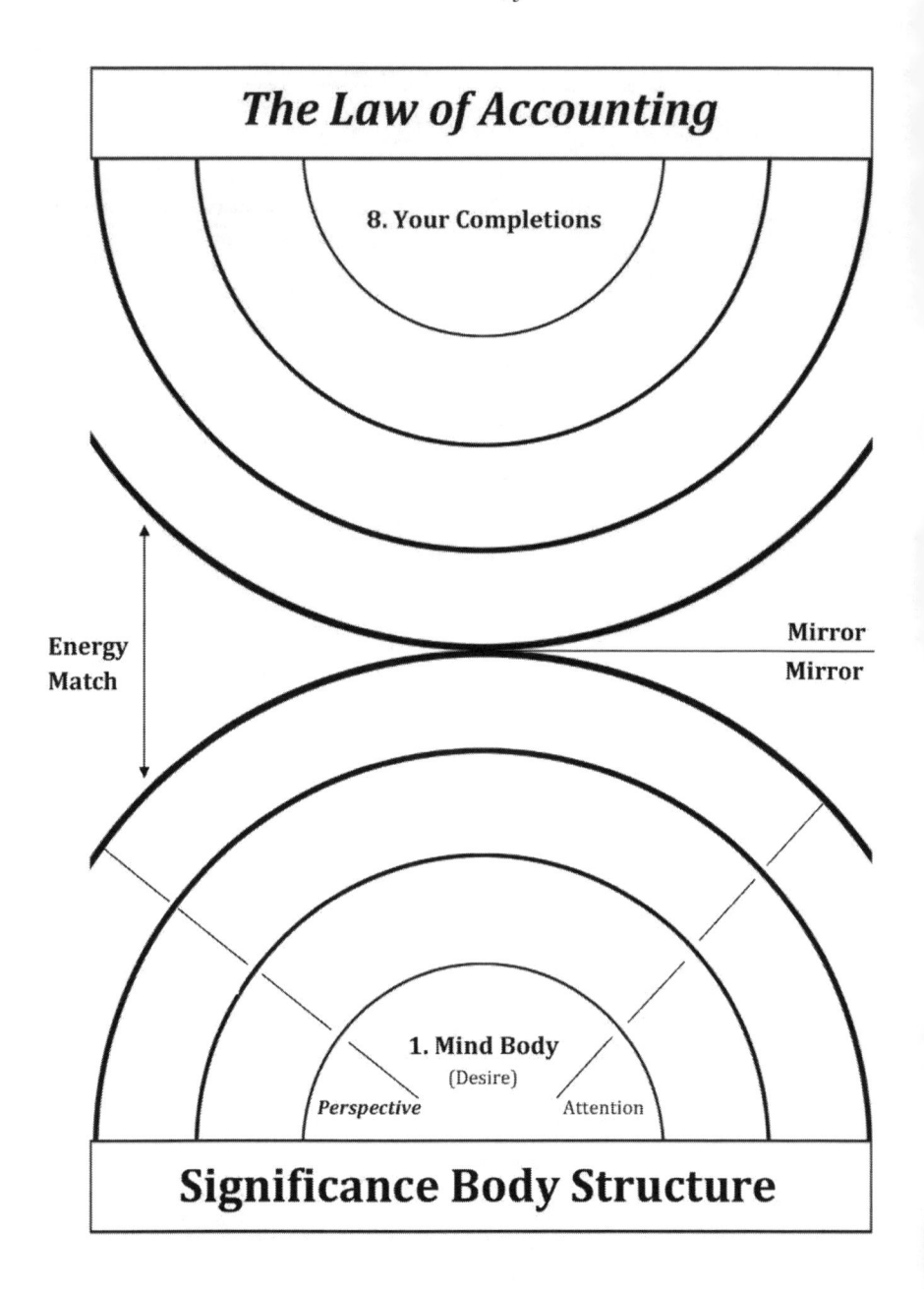

The Law of Accounting

8. Your Completions

Energy Match

Mirror
Mirror

1. Mind Body
(Desire)

Perspective Attention

Significance Body Structure

The Trees of Life – The Anatomy of Existence

So let's start with a tree and some facts about trees that will illuminate the definition of life. When you think of, maybe, an oak tree; a fully-grown tree that's maybe 200-300 years old. The oak tree is massive and provides many points of shade. Now think of the content of the oak tree in terms of its massiveness. Where did the oak tree derive its mass? You would think that because of its solidness and all of its components, which includes the roots, trunk, bark, branches, and leaves, you would think that the mass was derived from the solid ground around it. But this is not true. The ground around a tree is never displaced, so it does not provide the tree the substance of its solid parts.

The only variable in this equation is water. Yes. The tree gets the entirety of its mass from water. As water goes into the ground and is drawn in by the root system, it receives instructions to reform into solid parts as extending from current parts. All of these instructions were contained in a seed that eventually becomes a tree; instructions with water being pushed by energy to transform based on these instructions.

What's amazing is the paralleling principal of formulation as it concerns neurons in the brain, which are water with instructions being pushed to transform based on the instructions. Also an amazing fact to consider is that the neurons as they are formed in the brain looks exactly like trees with branches. The point I am making here is that you can see the same process of existence and life existing on many levels and dimensions, but carrying the exact same principals of energy and reality.

We can quickly understand that the seed and the tree are equivalent in its existence. The entirety of a tree abides in the seed. The seed carries invisible instruction that is set to push the water. Your thoughts are just like seeds. What is incredible about all this, here are seeds unlike seeds in nature, these "thought seeds" are designed to push water, but are widely variable based on what you and I want. A lemon tree seed will always produce lemon trees. An oak seed will always produce oak trees. An apple seed will always produce apple trees. But as humans we can originate seeds for multiple types of existences.

Your thoughts have the same developmental components as seeds.

You must clearly understand though that once a seed is born, it contains the entirety of its existence, and this entirety exists into infinity. Seeds are a source just as your thoughts are a source. The thought extends into infinity carrying with it the entirety of its existence. So there is no way to think a thought without the substance of that thought being fully in existence. Now just like the environment and an event, there is time that exist between the thought, which is energy, and the experience of that thought, which is the same energy. So life here is still about what is processed for experience. Life is about what you decide to remember. Future design can create memory just as well as past events can.

So there are several sources from which your thoughts spring. Not only must you monitor these sources, but you must monitor the resulting thoughts. With these thoughts being seeds that push water by giving water instructions, these seeds extend into infinity. Thoughts can never be taken lightly and must be managed, because in every thought is your end results.

Every thought contains end results. Here are the sources:

Natural Environment

Personal Desire or Direction

Investment From Others

Your Completions

Spirit - Inspiration

Sound – Timing, Rhythms, and Cycles
Rates of Accomplishments

Reflection – Biofeedback – Accounting

Memory

1. Natural Environment or Outside Events

Thoughts are formed as we assess what's outside of ourselves. Some people find themselves completely caught up in this environment of thinking.

2. Personal Desire or Direction

These are thoughts that originate from a source within us. We decide what these are. It's these thoughts where we must train ourselves to maintain as this becomes the basis of influencing how we process outside events and how the environment impacts us.

3. Investment from others.

Like the environment or outside events, these thoughts are derived from outside of us, but they stem from the environment of our relationships. But what's unique here is that your relationship environment is a controllable environment and a designable environment. Here are four quick things to use as a construct for your relationship environment.

      a. Intense Investment
      b. Intimate Action
      c. Integrity in Words Spoken
      d. Increasing Measurable Results

4. Your Completions

This is also environmental source where your thoughts originate from you, but these are your completions. As you convert thoughts from the form of invisible energy into physical energy that can be experienced, these same experiences are celebrated by new reflective thoughts that become extensions of the neuron trees within your brain.

5. Spirit – Inspiration

This is the most important origin of thoughts as it is the core of the Law of Accounting. The Universe itself extends from a seed or thought itself, and the entirety of the Universe contains all of its own completions. What fascinating about this, is that you being a result of the Universe and simultaneously a seed generator yourself, the entirety of the Universe is contained within you. The fact that you exist is its own proof. If you check back into your personal density, all of what you are extends back into infinity before beginnings. All of what you can be extends into the future into infinity. Everything you want to be, and everything you can ever want is accounted before you. Now obtaining anything you want in life becomes a matter of access, ability and more over, what you are awake to. Life, Energy is always there to supply your every thought. So listen.

6. Sound – Timing, Rhythms, and Cycles
   Rates of Accomplishments

Life is also a series of timings, rhythms, or cycles called frequencies. This is the only way to measure energy. Most energy cannot be seen, but as this energy floats around into infinity, it impacts the development of your thoughts. With certain frequencies or energy, just by you being in its presence, it can invoke new thought processes, but just like relationships, you can design this energy and you can control this energy.

7. Reflection – Biofeedback – Accounting

Reflection involves a combination of all these energies. Your beginnings, your endings, your environments, your processes, your surrounding energies, and of course your relationships all provide a pulse of reflection back towards yourself which acts as a biofeedback that reports back to you your aliveness.

8. Memory

Remember, you are the substance of things hoped for, and you are the evidence of things not seen. Your dreams, ideas, and desires, which are not seen, should not pose any psychological issues whatsoever. You are the substance for everything you want to be. You are the starting point. You just have to build advanced memory of what you want to experience. When this is done, the entirety of what you want reflects a present reality. When a desire exists in the mind and is focused on, it also exists in its entirety outside the mind. Its first formulation of existence is the neurons. Once this happens it's already done.

Desire here should be your main point of focus. This is where you build advance memory. All other of these eight points of resources for your thoughts actually relate back to your desire. Desire here is the only resource for thoughts that originate from you. You are the originator of life and you are also the point where life completes itself. Now become acutely aware of the substances that have been set in time for you to relate to that guarantees your results. You don't find these substances, you remember them.

The Law of Accounting

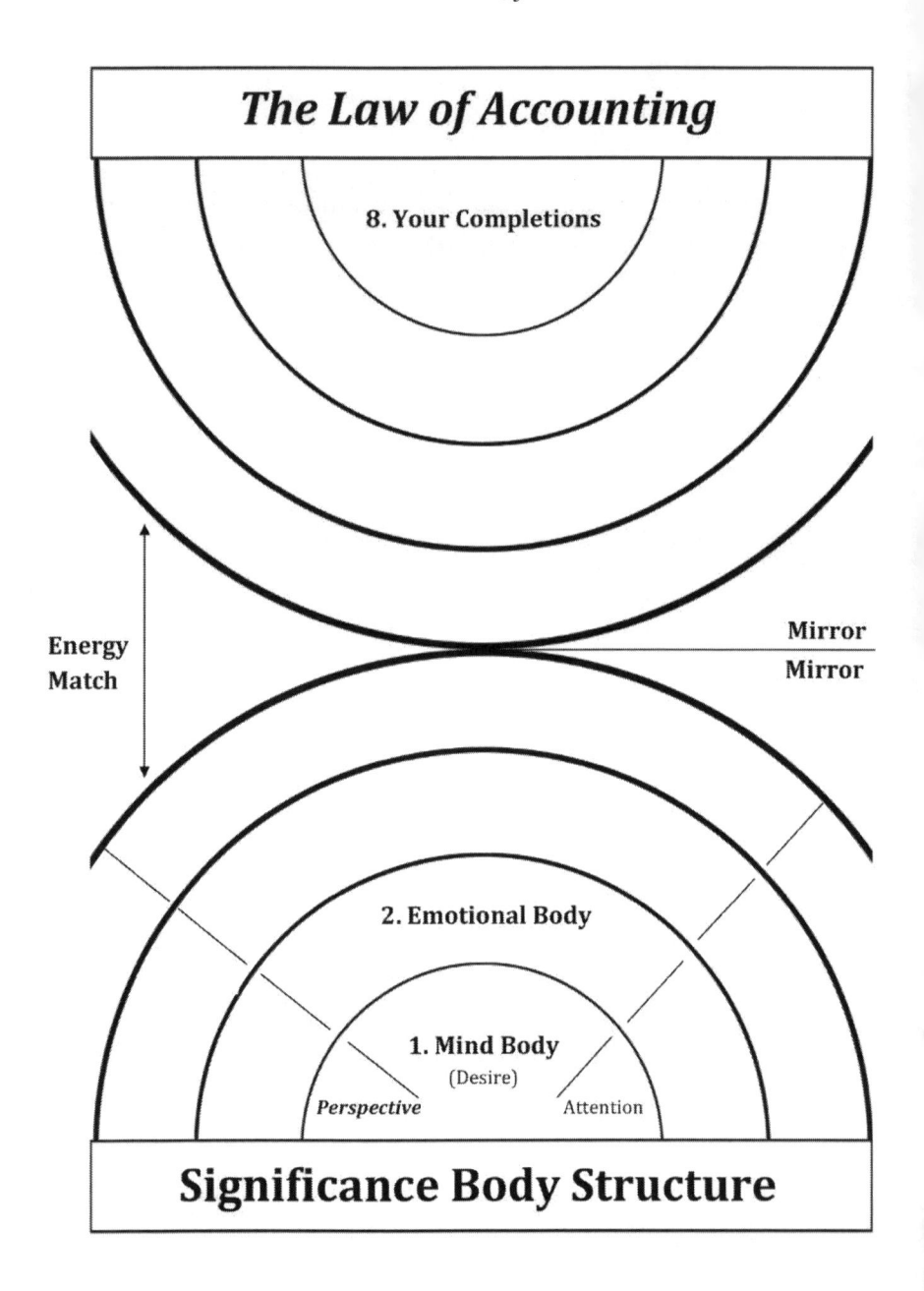

8. Your Completions

Energy Match

Mirror
Mirror

2. Emotional Body

1. Mind Body
(Desire)

Perspective — Attention

Significance Body Structure

The Emotional Body

The seat of significance is contained in your emotional body. At the end of the day, it all comes down to how you feel. How do you feel about yourself? How do you feel about what others think about you? This is the seat of significance. The emotional system is one of the most fascinating systems within the body. When you say that you feel something, what you are actually dealing with is the placement of a series chemicals in your body that is secreted throughout the body by the glands and your brain.

The short of it is that your glands secrete chemicals and these chemicals attach to receptors at the end of what is called protein strands. These protein strands pierce the cells in your body and when the chemicals make its attachment to these receptors, it sends a message to the brain saying, this is the way I feel. Emotions are all chemical processes and not necessarily how you actually feel. You just process these chemicals as a feeling.

Quite frankly, you can take one pill or some type of narcotic and immediately change your feelings. Better yet, you can take a pill or some type of narcotic and change the state of your body, and thusly change the state of your mind. This altered state and the ability to take a short cut to these states and new emotions is the basis of most addictions. As matter of fact, the topic of addiction is the best way to show you the power of your emotional system.

Emotions, Its all Chemicals

It can be easily said that the basis of most addiction is the feeling of insignificance, and most people are addicted to something that to them helps bring back some since of balance and significance. Comfort is a state that most people want to achieve, but as the brain constantly makes assessments about the state of life, it can race as the surrounding conditions shift. This is natural. In the end, the mind wants to experience significance.

I want to make a note here that what happens in the body chemically is mirrored from the mind as the neurons form based on life assessments or the processing of events that we discussed earlier. But what's unique about the chemical processes that take place within the body; once it is set, the body becomes many times more powerful than the mind. I tell people all the time, if you have a desire, in order to accomplish it, it must be built in the body first. This is what we meant earlier about training to create memory. You repeat an idea via practice until you feel it in your body. Once this is done, it becomes almost entirely impossible to change the mind. This works towards your success and your failures.

With a person who is suffering from addiction, he or she might have a desire to stop whatever repetitive behavior, but the body will always speak louder than the mind due to the simulated chemical set taken into the body externally. The body holds a vital role within life. The body becomes the most powerful reaction to your thoughts or your life assessments. Once these secreting glands respond to your thinking, you affect the state of your body and create bodily memory sets. You need to know, no matter how you see it, you never do what you plan to do, you only do what you remember as it is built in your body..

Once again, this all becomes a manipulation of water, h2o. You are further determining how energy and water reacts in order to create new substance within yourself. This is a process of creation. Addiction is a process of creation. When you fail at building anything substantive outside the body, you force creation inside the body via the hyper-creative process of taking external chemical substances.

The Substance of Things Hoped For

So let's look at the word substance that will help give clarity to what's happening here. Substance is the goal of life. Substance is the only way one can mirror life. The primary life process is for invisible energy to convert into physical usable energy that becomes a mirror to what can't be seen, the invisible. When this happens, it reports to the mind that all is ok. Any interruption in this process forces the question of why. When there is an inability to answer this question, a neurosis sets in. Then people spend a great deal of time trying resolve this neurosis, trying to resolve the feeing that something is missing, or trying to resolve the feeling of insignificance.

This is what bothers me about religion and spiritualist. The attempt here is to try to make the invisible the optimal state of life. Somehow, what is on the other side of physical reality or the physical side of energy is more important than substantive existences. When this is done, there is a natural devaluation of the self, because the self is one's experience, and you cannot have experience without substance. This is the problem when people promote God as the answer to all of life's problems. This is funny, when God is promoting you as the answer to life's problems.

As I mentioned early on, we are not dealing with filling empty space. There is no such thing as empty space. So one would promote, let God fill this space and you will be ok. Notice, the country that has the largest "spiritual" or "religious" population also has the greatest substance abuse problem. So I must say again, you are the substance of things hoped for. What is hoped for? More substance. An addict has just found a shortcut to at least make the body feel accomplished.

The Evidence of Things not Seen

In actuality, there is no such thing as addiction. There is no such thing as an addict. There is only accomplishment and the sense of accomplishment. If you want to use the words addict or addiction, then every human on earth has an addiction or is addicted to something. The difference is there is just a law against some and no laws against others. I'll start here. Let's list the following illegal substances:

1. Cocaine
2. Heroin
3. Cannabis or Weed
4. Meth
5. Alcohol
6. Ecstasy
7. Prescription Drugs

These seven are enough to make my point. Now I will list one legal substance:

1.   Sugar

Because of sugar alone, I've seen people who have had their feet amputated, and people who have had both legs amputated. I've seen people who have gone blind. I've seen where the inflammation caused by sugar cause heart attacks and strokes. How many people can actually stop using sugar? Here, I am just scratching the surface of unnoticed "addictions". What's happening here again, is not addiction, but repeated attempts at creation. The human mind and body is geared towards winning, success, and accomplishment. Substance abuse is just a mode of this effort.

The problem of external chemical intake to obtain a certain emotional balance or euphoria is that the sensorium or feelings created as a result stem from just that, a small pill, crystals, powder, smoke, or a drink. With this, substance abuse, there is no true mirrored existence to match the feeling. This also illuminates other outside a stimulus that leaves you in the same state of having no mirrored substantive existences to match the euphoria, such as events and people. Once interacted with, these same evens and people leave you with only a sense of significance, but after a very short while, insignificance sets in because there is no true creation of something substantive. People get high off of other people, relationships, religious experiences, and other events. Here, the evidence of things hoped for becomes highly elusive, allusive, and illusive. Here again, we are not dealing with emptiness, but distance.

The Substance of Sound

Now, I have to deal with the first relationship component of life or life creation. It is sound. Mainly sound or words that come from others. Sound, being a form of energy is the most acute action that directly affects neuron creation in the brain and chemical creation in the body. Life is a matter of connection, and when there is no connection there is disconnection. Disconnection signifies distance and not emptiness. Insignificance is really more associated with distance. So the proper response to insignificance is closing distance.

Here is where sound can become dangerous. Sound is the most accurate structuring tool of the neurons and chemical sets in the body. Sound is the most moving because sound in itself is motion. So the mind and the body more readily respond to sound than any other thing. But all sound must be followed by action and results in order for the sound to be authenticated. Otherwise sound can become your biggest drug. This is why there is a necessity for integrity.

When somebody speaks to you any type of commitment, hope is immediately set in, but hope without evidence is horrifying because immediate distance is set within the mind and body. What's unique about sound and words is your mind and body will accept it as truth and reality. When you tell somebody that you will do something, it registers in the mind and body as being completed. When somebody tells you something in terms of commitment, it doesn't register in the mind and body as something that will be done, it registers as already done.

This is why music is the most constructive energy in existence. Every athlete does not perform without it, every businessperson listens to it as they're forging his or her goals and destination; every movie, and every commercial uses its power. Every surgeon has it to accompany his or her surgery. Every grocery store, retail chain, mall and restaurant plays it while you make you're purchasing decisions. Every church, religion, and spiritual institution employs its power to create optimal experiences. Physical fitness experts dare not include music in their routine. People jog and exercise to music, shower to music, and work to music.

You must learn to hear your agreements.

The power of sound. Spoken words are definitely more constructive. So what you need to hear is your agreements. This is your first clue as to whether the words people are speaking to you or around you is a drug like phenomenon or actually words that play a real role in creation and building results. Their vocal investment must agree with your direction. A lot of us spend a great deal of time listening to crap. So you must be vigilant in the placement of personages around you that can speak in line with the energy of your desire and direction. This is the first component of building right relationships. Think of the relationships you build as a band that will supply you with your life's music. All of your relationships are a literal playlist like on an I-pod and Mp3 player that play into you who you're going to be.

Sound Strategies

1. Keep a playlist on your Mp3 player, I-pod, I-pad, PC tablet, cellphone, etc. in line with your personal desire and direction.
2. Have music composed specifically for your success.
3. Keep the individuals that you connect with that only speak towards your improvement.
4. Keep your word and fire those around you who have a hard time keeping their word.

The Law of Accounting

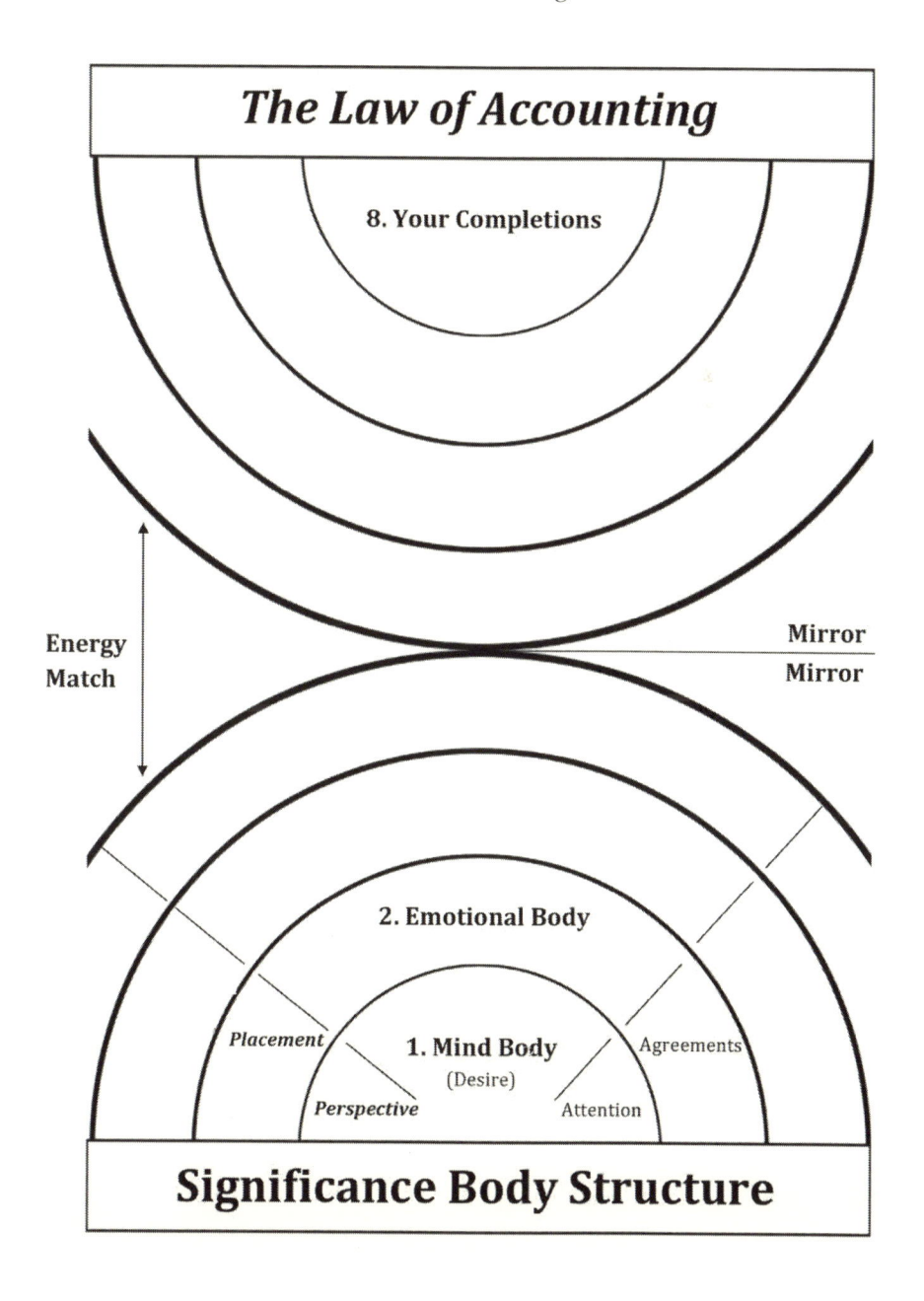

8. Your Completions

Energy Match

Mirror
Mirror

2. Emotional Body

Placement

1. Mind Body
(Desire)

Agreements

Perspective

Attention

Significance Body Structure

Placements

So here, you must give an account for your placement of people around you and your agreements. Your personal placement of personages becomes a feeder to your emotional systems. The chemicals in your body are highly responsive to the people you associate with. When you are making a decision to move forward, for example, and everything in you is not allowing you to do just that, you might ask the question, "What's wrong with me?". The feelings inside you are out of sorts. To resolve the emotional turmoil, you have to begin to account for the personages around you. The construct of the personages around you becomes the construct of the chemicals within. Taking pills or drugs to manipulate your chemical condition does not change this. It is within our relationships that we do the least work.

The construct of your emotional body system becomes vital because it is this very same system that acts as an antenna to the like energy around you. Again, this not the Law of Attraction, but this is the Law of Supply. If your emotional system is set to disappointment, you can walk into room of 15 people; fourteen of those people are people that can help you with your dream, one person in the room can only bring more disappointment; then out of all those people you speak to, the one that brings more disappointment is the one you lock in. It is not that you attracted that person to you. Fourteen others were there to help you with your dream. You were just in tune with what was already within you.

If you want to change the bad feelings, which can only tune you in and produce more bad, change the people around you. This change alone will open your eyes to whole new worlds of what's actually present to you for your success.

The Relationship Accounts Body

So, I would like to remind you that even though we are discussing a total of eight bodies, all eight bodies are one body. I might say, as I get to each body, that this is the most important body on the chart, in actuality; all the bodies are equally vital. But I really want to say that your Relationship Accounts Body is the most important part your body. The Law of Accounting stems out of this one major truth, and that's the truth of everything you can imagine or create within your mind already exist and is present to you. By default, this has been counted before you much like a guarantee. Everyone on earth is actually equally successful whether you realize it or not. The difference is, is what's accounted for.

People who appear to be more successful in life or more accomplished in life are really people who are capable of accounting for what's already been assigned to them. Life is about accounting or taking an account. Those who can do it better, live better. It's as simple as that. Every last human on earth has been equally assigned fullness, but not everyone is capable of living his or her fullness. This all flows back into what you and I take an account for. This chart of the Law of Accounting gives you a little known map of what to account for. This Relationship Accounts Body is the least worked on.

The Law of Accounting

8. Your Completions

Energy Match

Mirror
Mirror

3. Relationship Accounts

2. Emotional Body

Placement

1. Mind Body
(Desire)

Agreements

Perspective

Attention

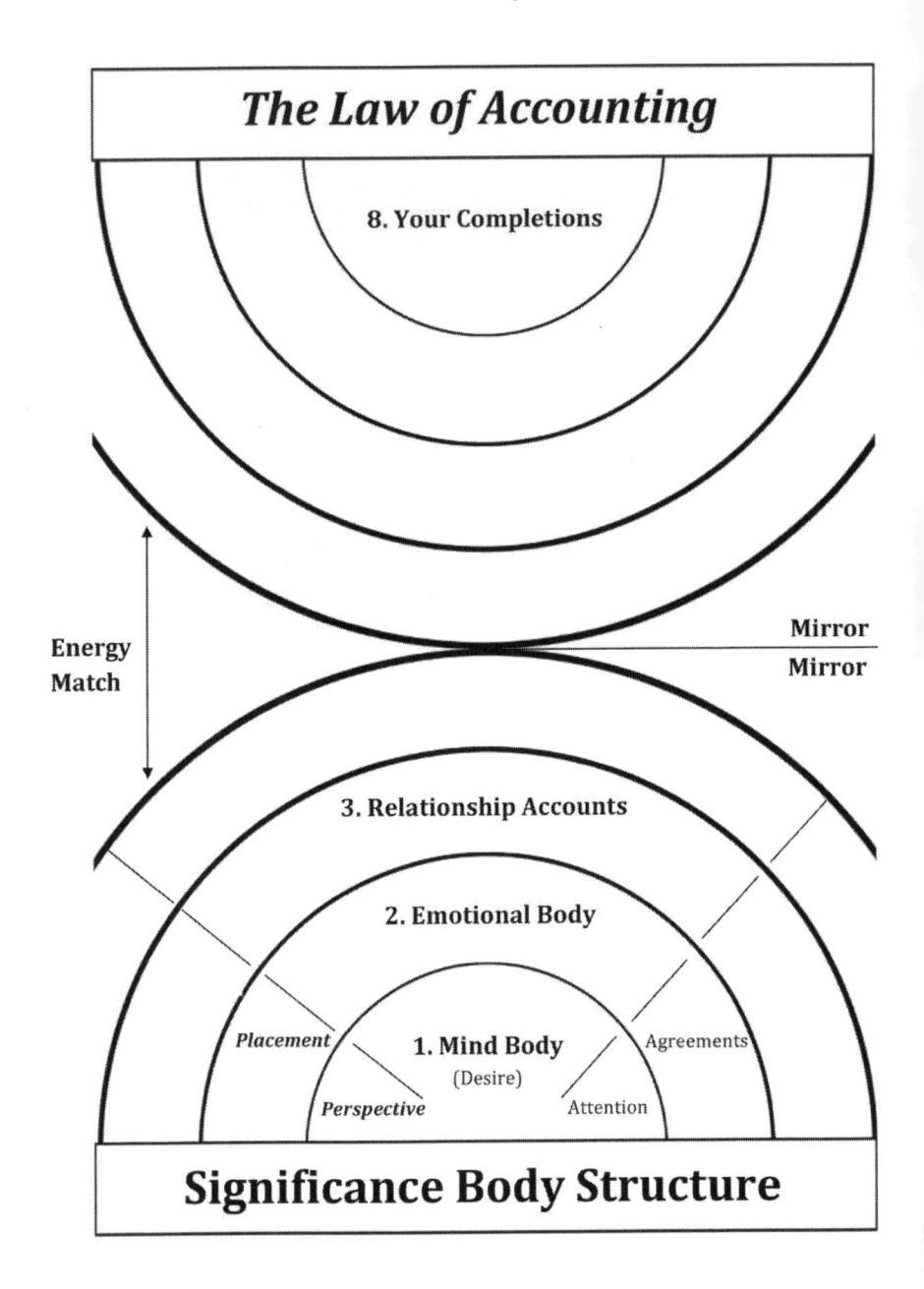

Significance Body Structure

The Corporate World Has it Right

A business is in business to produce results. To make a business work, there has to be a series of relationships. It is usually the CEO of a company that cast the vision and goals of the company. The CEO immediately has along side of him or her other C-level executives that he or she can count on to initiate and manage the directives of the CEO. You might then have a chief operating officer or a chief financial officer that operate within their respective roles. Supporting them are company directors. Then under the directors might be the department managers, and under the managers you have the employees.

Each company has a directive, which is their end-goals or their products and services. When the CEO mandates a directive, instructions are given and the respective company lineup follows suit in order to produce a specific result. There is an accounting on every level. Whoever is underperforming, the underperformance is not tolerated or else the end result is not reached.

It should work the exact same way with your relationships. First, you must have a directive. You must have a dream or a desire; otherwise your relationships will never work without it. Remember, as I said earlier, a relationship within itself should never be an end goal or your point of desire. You should have a desire, dream, or some type of directive and then your relationships should be subsequent to that. Have you ever seen a company or a business hire all its staff and employees, and then try to determine the goals of the company? No. Never.

Neither will your relationships work without you having specific desires or destinations set for yourself. Moreover, anyone who underperforms or doesn't perform accordingly is fired. The same goes for an orchestra or a band; a band director cannot possibly or even remotely tolerate any band member playing a wrong note, or playing the wrong rhythm. What if a band member decided to play an entirely different song than the other band members? Even if it is as simple a band member being out of tune, he or she is immediately corrected.

So here, we have this thing called life, and we don't even come close to requiring the same type of accounting within our relationships. A person stepping to you for any type or level of relationship must:

1. Always be aware of what you want to accomplish in life.
2. Have some type of skill set that enables them to offer you something towards that.
3. Commit to serving your end goals.
4. Follow through with intimate action.
5. Have measurable results that you can count on.

This should be the basis of every relationship including blood relatives. If a mother does not feed her baby as required, she would be charged with a crime. People listen! To be in relationship with people who are in any way unsupportive, lack support, or even has an inability to support you is criminal in nature! Because within this, there is psychological robbery and murder consistently taking place. Somehow, this is made to be ok, because the notion is, based on the fact that the relationship itself is the end goal, the notion is "work it out". No! When someone has broken into your house while you are there and proceeds to pack up all your stuff, you do not begin to work out an arrangement with the burglar, you call 911. Without accountable action towards you, you are either being robbed or dying, most likely both. What's sad is when a person stamps the label of "love" on top this.

You can want to date this person or that person, be in love with this person or that person, want this person or that person, or don't want to lose this person or that person; but never hold anybody to any type of standard or have them to give an account to your own well being. Your Relationship Accounts Body is just that, it is part of your body of existence, but yet most do not give this body an account. The reason why people find themselves so damaged is due mainly to damaged relationships that go under-recognized. Let's look at the next part.

The Law of Accounting

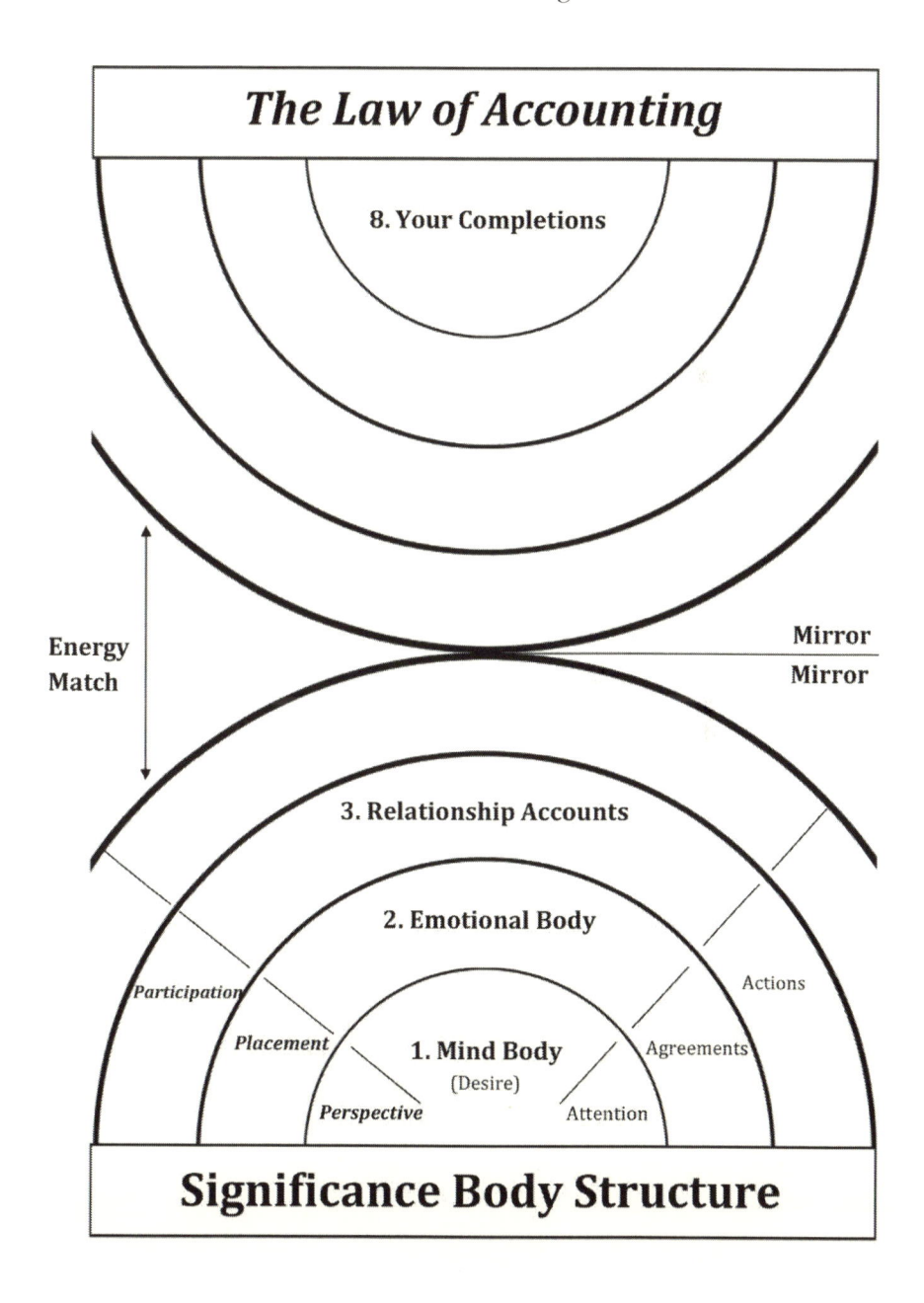

8. Your Completions

Energy Match

Mirror
Mirror

3. Relationship Accounts

2. Emotional Body

Participation

Placement

1. Mind Body
(Desire)

Perspective

Actions

Agreements

Attention

Significance Body Structure

Intimate Action and Integrity

These should be the chief requirements to any relationship, intimate action and integrity. Sometimes because of "love", using the word "requirement" when it comes to a relationship might make some cringe. For the most part, when it comes to any type of relationship, we know what we want out of the relationship, but have a very difficult time in transferring those "wants" into requirements. To fully understand this we have to go back to how the chemicals work in the body.

When one says he or she is "in love", it is not recognized that we are dealing with a feeling which is just a chemical component in the body. No, I am not reducing love to a mere chemical component. What I am doing is telling you that the chemical component that signifies what most people think is love is not love at all. Chemicals in your body that come across as feelings are not feelings but signals, much like a traffic light. Emotions such as fear, anger, discontent, and the like are generally treated as stop-lights. Emotions such as love, joy, and excitement are generally treated as go-lights.

I hear it all the time, "I'm in love". A person can list out a laundry list of bad treatment experienced by the one they are in a relationship with, but still can feel totally "in love" with that person. There is no matching between the "feeling" of love and the behavior of the other person. But the feeling of love here becomes the go light without the person having to fulfill any requirements that constitute real love. The feeling only is considered as the entirety of love. I love him. I love her. I am in love with him. I am in love with her. This becomes enough for intimate action. Bad move. Let me help you here.

Love should never be the signal for intimate action; love should only be a result of intimate action. Again we treat this emotion or chemical as a signal to move forward and not allow for true love or true actions to create the chemical or emotion. Just seeing the person becomes enough, or more dangerously, just hearing the person becomes enough. Any love that doesn't extend out of intimate action becomes an illusion that leads to delusion, but then, you become the only one taking all the action to match your emotion. All you are doing here is following the direction of a mere chemical in your body and ignoring the behavior pattern of the one that you are "in love" with. Let me help you with this.

Love should only be a result of intimate action.

What you hear (sound) and what is acted out must be the same thing. If it's different, it is not love.

Closing the Distance

Remember when I said when a person is feeling empty, they are not actually empty, they are only at a distance. When a person has been mistreated in the past, misrepresented in the past, or left alone in the past, rejected in the past, or even abandoned in the past, a distance is created in the body. This is why I said, and will say, REALTIONSHIPS ARE A PART OF YOUR BODY. This distance is formulated as a chemical that matches or mirrors the distance created from the unfortunate event. From this instant, a desire is formed to close the distance. Pay close attention here.

A desire should denote creativity. This inevitably becomes the strongest desire, because it exists within the body. This desire is a living existence. What should be ensued by the desire is the creation of the "thing" that closes the distance. What should be ensued by the desire is creation. Creation should and is the correct movement that should always accompany desire.

Let's take a young lady that is in this position. That desire becomes a chemical in the body, which is love within the body before it becomes love outside the body. With this, creation should ensue. But remember this chemical is treated as a traffic light and not a point of creation. So when the first guy comes along, she uses the guy to close the distance versus using the guy to create a relationship. The chemical, because it is now defined as love, says "go" when the chemical actually should say "create".

1.	Desire	1.	Desire
2.	Create	2.	Connect to the creation

It is the actions of the guy that should close the distance and not the mere presence of the guy. There are no requirements for creation. The internal desire of the young lady is transformed into the desire for the guy only. It is an erroneous existence to desire another person. That desire is then defined as love without the guy having to do anything at all.

So with this notion, we have many relationships without creation. They just exist without production. Being "in love" is not good enough. If we can slow the mind down enough, all the tragedies of the past can be reformed into creations for the future. But what we generally do is take that same desire that's birthed out of a past tragedy and assign it to an individual, versus taking that individual and giving them assignments. What needs to be done here is stop saying "I love you", before saying "Here's what you can do for me". Here you are not choosing a person to fill a black hole from the past, but you are connecting to a person to accomplish a future designed desire, which in itself diminishes the past. Creation cannot happen otherwise. Saying "I love you" is never noble without some type of active practice. Remember, you cannot create good memory in the body without practice.

Integrity

When someone gives you their word, you must know your mind does not know the difference between what a person says and what a person does. When someone says something to you, it exist in reality immediately, because neurons form in your brain off of words and sound as well as actions. When someone does not complete an action based on his or her word, new distance is also created within the mind and the body.

It's amazing how we keep people around that keep telling us stuff over and over again without any follow-up with action. This is because the words and sound can make you feel complete within itself. Back to a young lady in this position, all the guy has to do is keep talking or making new promises. He is then good to go. Then it's usually the young lady that ends up taking the most actions, which is based on her desire for the individual and not anything he has done.

Within a corporate structure, integrity is a must, but within the context of a relationship it is not as nearly focused on. We want to believe what a person says. If that same person said the same crap to their boss and did not follow through, they will be immediately fired, because a business cannot afford for commitments to made and not followed up. You cannot afford it either, but sometimes pay the price again and again for words spoken and action not taken. You must become professional in your relationships. You must require active commitments; otherwise you are contributing to your own insignificance.

You must become a professional in your relationships.

The idea of accounting is about security. You should feel secure when someone speaks to you. You should have a masterful sense that something will get done because one said so. If this is not the case, you will lose your sense of timing and cycles.

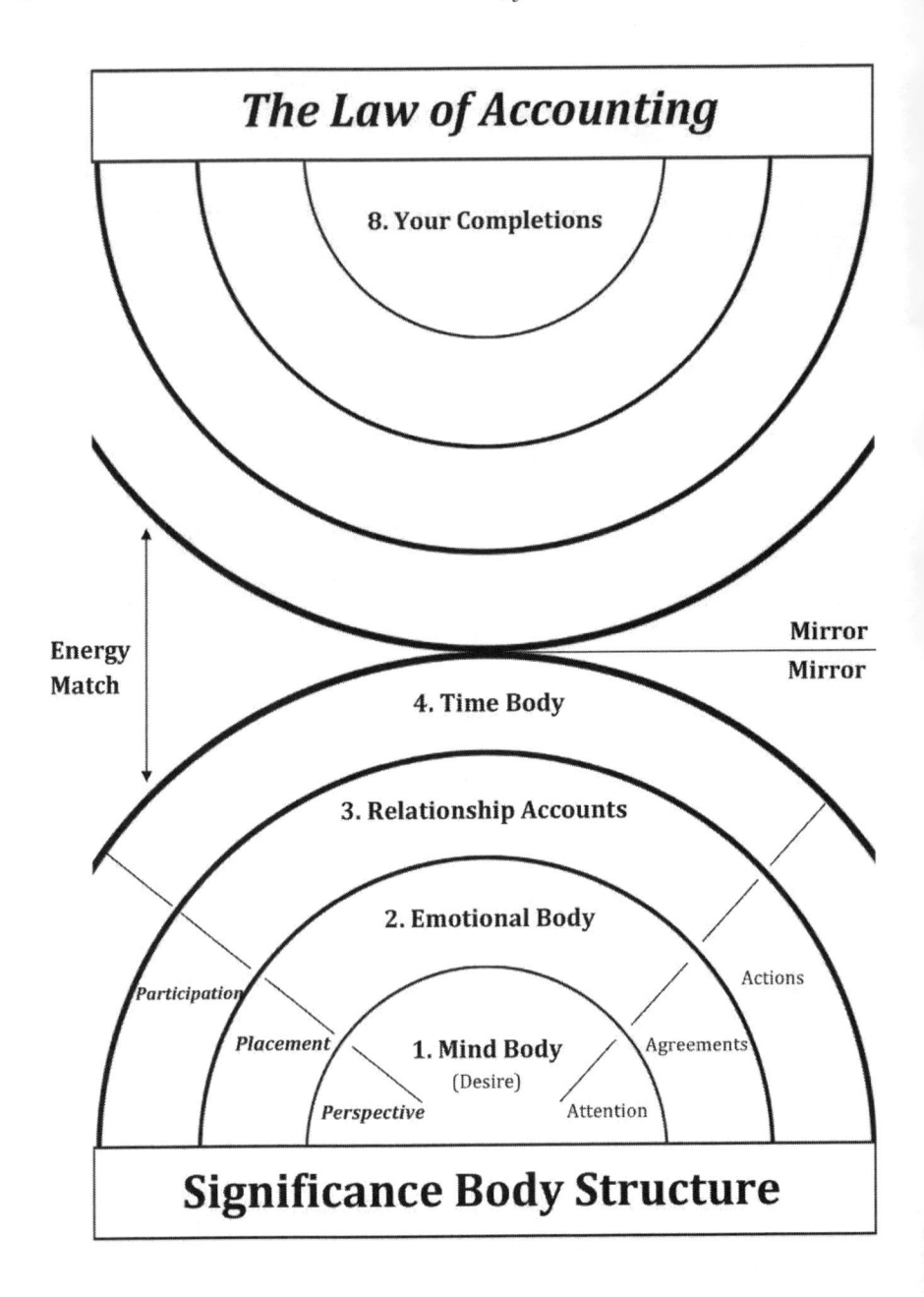

The Law of Accounting

8. Your Completions

Energy Match

Mirror
Mirror

4. Time Body

3. Relationship Accounts

2. Emotional Body

Actions

Participation

Placement

1. Mind Body
(Desire)

Agreements

Perspective

Attention

Significance Body Structure

Time Body – Your Outer Mirror

One of the most important components of your personal significance is knowing your seasons, cycles, and knowing when things are to be produced in your life. This is being aware of your timing and your cycles. The key to the Law of Accounting is having the awareness that everything desired is immediately accomplished, but the placement of your accomplishment for experience happens based on how you handle time and you understanding the energy of time.

The best way to illuminate this truth is for you to understand how a bankcard to a bank account works. A bankcard gives you access to your money within a particular bank. So time here is about access, access to your accomplishments. When it comes to a bankcard, what's in your bank account is directly mirrored on the bankcard. What you produce in life is directly mirrored from what's inside you. The people you associate with or your relationships represent your bankcard. Let's graph it so we can get a clear picture.

1. Your Bank Account = What's Inside You
2. Bank Card = Your Relationships
3. Access to Money = Your Accomplishments

The point of time is about accessing what you want to accomplish in life. It exists, so how do you access your desired end points. So, how does your timing or cycles work within all of this? I'll start with the bankcard. For the most part because of technology, bankcards work instantaneously. But what you must realize, just a few years ago, there was no such thing as a bankcard. You had to write a check to access your money if you were away from your bank. In this scenario, a check takes several days to process. So you have the same process between a bankcard and a check, but two different timing scenarios between them. The state of your relationships scales the timing of your accomplishments, and it also affects the end points of your accomplishments differently on the basis of a person's credit list:

Credit List

1. Their consciousness of your end game.
2. Their consciousness of what your needs are.
3. Their level of communication towards you.
4. Their level of attention towards your details.
5. Their level of understanding of what you want.
6. Their connection to your desire or results.
7. Their willingness to commit.
8. The past experience in their past commitments.
9. Their ability to commit.
10. Their commitment as shown through their actions.

As your stuff passes through others just like a bankcard or a hand written check, it determines the timing and the placement of your results. The better a person fits the criteria of this list, the quicker your results come into existence. Let me be clear, results are enabled only through partnerships just like financial flow is enabled by a bankcard.

Now, to better understand how the Law of Accounting works, you have to consider the energy of what you want. Then you have to consider how the energy of what you want and how it relates to the energy of the Universe. The desire, which comes first and emanates from a thought, is pure energy. The brain becomes the manufacturing plant for your thought energy. Then the body becomes the second manufacturing plant of that same energy push. Your glands immediately respond to the advent of a thought as well as the advent of the responding neurons.

What happens here, as your body serves as an antenna, the Universe responds to the totality of the energy that has been committed within your body. What the Universe does faithfully is channel out the energy of what you want out to every possible resource in existence, which was and always will be available for your accounting. The Universe is not expanding by happenstance, but it is in a continuous state of provision by unfolding sounding energies and frequencies in response to your creative thought. This is why it becomes vital, that once your have a desire, you have to train your body until that desire becomes fully alive in your body. This is done so as distractions are presented, your desire is so locked in, your body continues to enforce intense focus.

We do know that the human body is electrical in nature. If it weren't so, your finger touching your cell phone or tablet would not have any affect. There is then a relationship of this bodily electricity to water, which comprises a majority of your body. Your thoughts manipulate your body systems in a very intricate way, influencing the creation of chemicals, which are your emotions. This chemical structure arises out of the water, just like the neurons arises out of the water and electricity which creates a unique energy system. This is all electrical in nature. Energy in motion. The motion of this energy is called a frequency.

Frequency and Time

There are 12 main frequencies that make up the Universe, much like the 12 notes that comprises the musical tones on most instruments. From ancient mankind to the present, both scientist and non-scientist have read these 12 frequencies as astrological houses. You can consider these houses as states of energy depending on where the earth and planets are in tandem to the sun at any given time. This is where we get our since of time, our 365 days a year, our 12 months, and our 24 hour time construct based on the earth's rotation in relation to the sun. So what we really are dealing with here as we consider time, it is not time at all, but the placement of energy. When you set a desire, the next is that desire comes into reality, which is simply the placement or arrangement of energy within the earth.

This placement of energy also gives us the construct of our four seasons, and it is natural knowledge that different things that's done are optimal within different seasons. We read all of this stuff based on its cycles within time, which is simply frequency. The earth has it's own frequency as well as the sun, along with every planet and star in the Universe. Are these frequencies happenstance or design?

Again most read the 12 main frequencies of the Universe from an astrological standpoint, but they can also be read from a musical standpoint since these frequencies are parallel to the same notes that show up in our musical system. Every music tone has its own frequency and is an accurate representation of the Universal frequencies. So I am going to turn this and the truth will remain. The 12 astrological frequencies or zodiac houses are an accurate representation of the 12 musical tones, not the other way around.

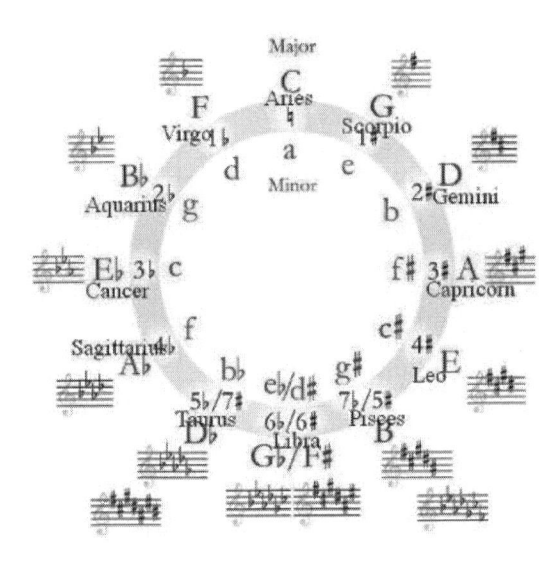

What you would need to know is that your body is emanating a continuous energy presence that is also frequency based. The body itself contains its own energy plant that controls the movement and the health of your cells called the lymphatic system. The resulting energy of the body connects with outside energies that affect your daily performance. Now it's easy to understand and get this stuff when it comes to satellite signals, cell phone towers, and the like, but we allow it to get muddy or we don't even consider it when it comes to our own personal energy. Your personal energy affects and moves energy outside of your body on a Universal scale, because it is all the same energy. When you touch your cellphone screen, you are manipulating energy. When you make a decision, likewise, you are manipulating energy. This is why you have to start accounting for how your energy is transcribed from you.

Let's get back to the 12 notes. Most see the zodiac houses as 12 energies that affect the happenings here on earth, and to a degree this is entirely correct. But that's a limited understanding of these 12 energy vortexes. A whole industry exist based on the zodiac houses as it is used to determine energy formulations according to the time a person is born on earth. But from a musical standpoint, these same houses can be considered as energy strings that are played by the energy of your thought compositions. When you think, the entirety of the Universe responds on multiple levels and dimensions just like a guitar responds to your fingers ran across its strings.

To put it best, every human on earth is a musician, whether they know it or not. Your behavior, your movements, and your thoughts play the Universe like a piano or a guitar. So you cannot only see the 12 zodiac houses as an influence on the earth's energy, but you precede the 12 houses as an influence on it. Most read the zodiac to determine how it's affecting their lives on earth, but it is more accurate to read the zodiac to strategize what notes you will play in life to assure and ensure your own accomplishments. So the 12 houses then become a personal development tool versus a tool for prediction.

The Sound of Time

So there it is, your thoughts are never local, but universal. Life is about production. Your thoughts coming from an invisible space into a living space governed by time and cycles. The reason why all this energy exists, the reason why all this sound is placed, is so that things can move from what can't be seen and then produced into what can be seen and thusly experienced. When you consider time in all of this, you are considering the cycle or cycles that exists in order to make things happen.

When you want to make something happen and you have in front of you something that you would like to accomplish, I would like for you to consider the cycles and not necessarily traditional time. Cycles more align with the concept of energy and frequencies. As matter of fact, traditional time is an elementary approach to accomplishment. Here, goal setting and putting things on a calendar has been the traditional strategy in terms of setting yourself up for accomplishment. Very few have been able to maintain a goal oriented trajectory using this model.

What you want to do here is to put your desire, direction, or dream into a cycle and then you look for measured production at different stages of the cycle. This helps you to mirror universal laws because this is how the rest of the universe functions. In the universe you have cycles and not necessarily time. The calendar here on earth does not work on Mars, or Neptune, or Venus, so it definitely won't work in other solar systems and galaxies. So, can you see how limiting time setting on our traditional calendar can be? From a standpoint of cycling, the cycles of energy begin within your mind and body, then cycles from there to your relationships. By now your accomplishments will be set in time by the energy of your cycles, and not setting the time on a calendar and then trying to set the energy.

1. Bodily Cycles = Time
2. Relationship Cycles = Time
3. Production Cycles = Time

So you have to pay attention to the energy of what you want. Since it is energy, this energy, being a frequency, has it's own cycles. So let's say you want a crop of corn and it's January. Your goal is to have stalks and ears of corn by July. You plant the corn in January, and then when July comes you will never see the corn. Why? You can't plant corn in January; the energy of the corn seed, or the cycle of the seed does not fit and so it is, many people make plans and it never happens. This is because they never considered the energy of what they want. People make calendar plans, but they don't make universally cycled plans.

So, your idea is like a seed. When a seed is planted in the right season and nurtured, it will produce exacting results. Your relationships are like the ground wherein a seed is planted. You must check the season of individuals you tie into and the nurturing capabilities of the personages you exchange with. Here, the music and the astrological charts can assist you in identifying that level of energy existence. Where are you planting your seeds? Does the person provide you with the right seasonal mix for planting? All this will affect the timing of your productions. Then the individual, much like a bankcard, must accurately represent what's within you. You do not want to swipe that card and it comes up with insufficient funds.

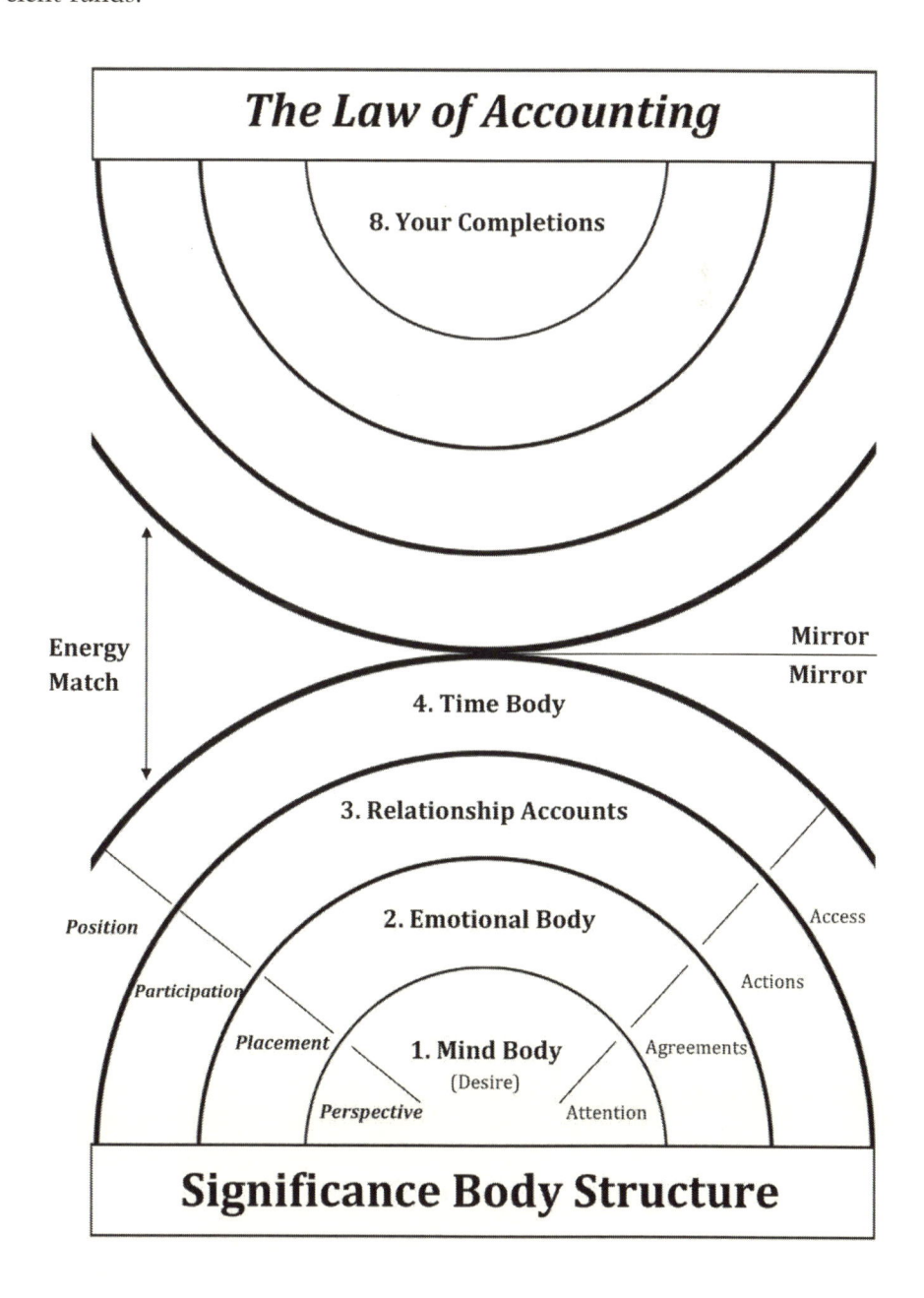

The Law of Accounting

- 8. Your Completions
- 4. Time Body
- 3. Relationship Accounts
- 2. Emotional Body
- 1. Mind Body (Desire)

Energy Match

Mirror / Mirror

Position, Participation, Placement, Perspective

Access, Actions, Agreements, Attention

Significance Body Structure

So here are some strategies to start:

1. Do not set your plans in time first. Build your plans in your body, initiate the cycles
2. The next cycle of your purpose is the relationships created around it.

   a. The better you choose here based on the list of ten things provided earlier, the quicker the partnership or relationship produces results.
   b. Your idea must be authenticated by experienced dedicated connections.
   c. Check the seasonal context of the energies based on who that person is.
   d. Check the seasonal content of the energies of the person.

3. Document your purpose as well as documenting the corresponding relationships.
4. Then you can use the traditional calendar to set local times.
5. Take measurements at different cycle points.

Under this, you will more congruently line up with the energies of Universal provisions, which creates a momentum of accomplishment that will far exceed your expectations. Time will then work on your behalf and time here, gives you access to consistent results. These results are the outer mirror of the content that exist within you. You can always check your outer mirror with your inner mirror.

The Law of Accounting

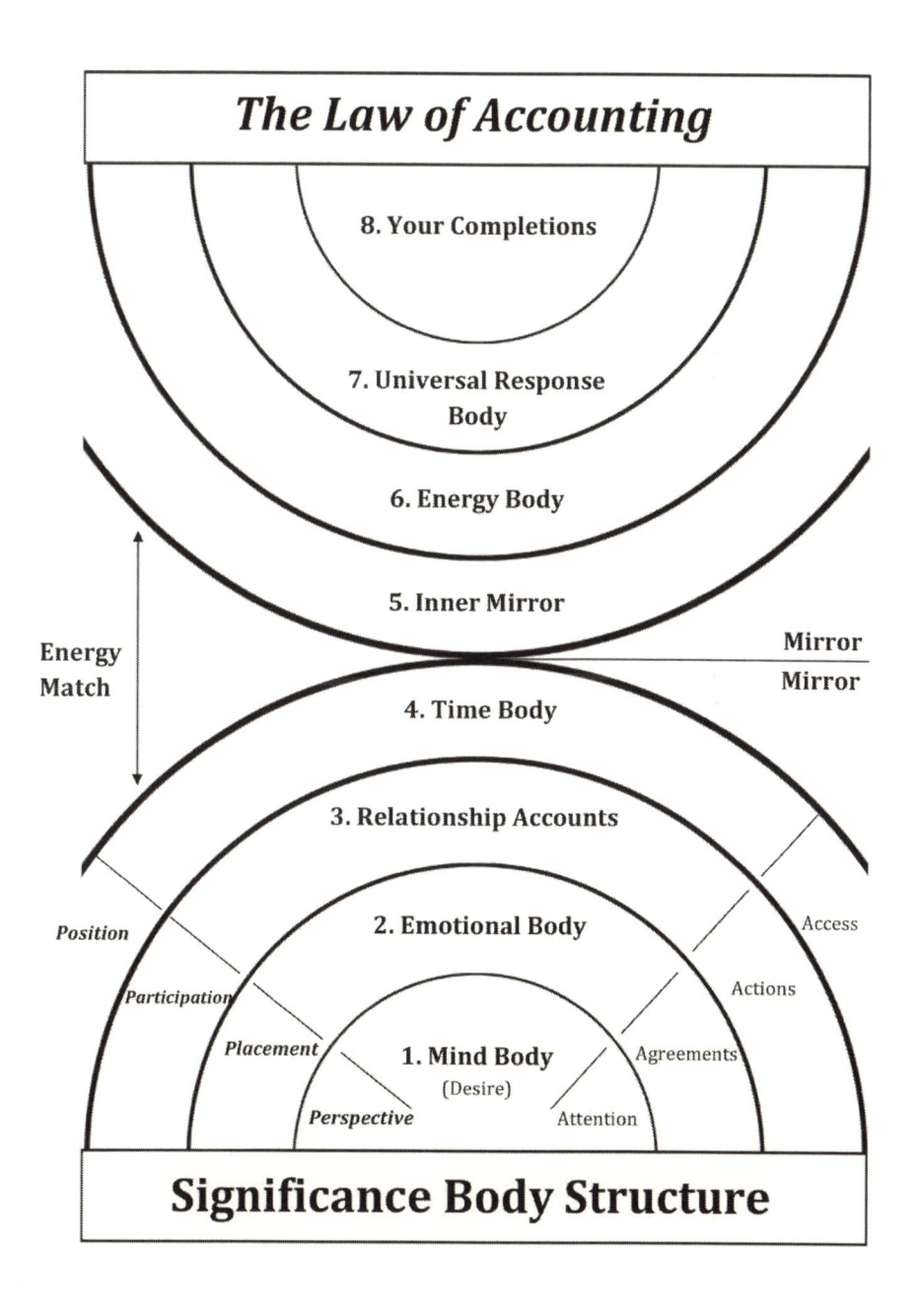

8. Your Completions

7. Universal Response Body

6. Energy Body

5. Inner Mirror

Mirror
Mirror

Energy Match

4. Time Body

3. Relationship Accounts

Position

2. Emotional Body

Access

Participation

Actions

Placement

1. Mind Body
(Desire)

Agreements

Perspective   *Attention*

Significance Body Structure

Your Inner Mirror, Your Energy Body, and Your Universal Response Body

The next four parts of your significance body are reflective of the first four.

Inner Mirror = Time

Energy Body = Relationships Account Body

Universal Response Body = Emotional Body

Completions Body = Mind Body

Let's reverse it:

Time = Inner Mirror

Relationships Accounts Body = Body

Emotional Body = Universal Response Body

Mind Body = Completion Body

The four initial bodies are the bodies we take action in and are personally responsible. The next four are a reflection of the first four, but is Universally responsible. The last four bodies are set as a guarantee to the first four bodies. The last four bodies are also a Universal provision for the first four bodies. As I said, you are fully provided for, and for every desire there is full supply for that desire.

Inner Mirror - Spirit Body

The inner mirror represents your access to full knowledge. Most refer to this inner mirror as your inner spirit. Christians refer to this inner mirror as the Holy Spirit. Whatever the case, full knowledge is always available to access for direction. This knowledge mirrors your desires in the form of information. If you ever thought about the instructions found within any type of seed that pushes water into a multiplicity of forms, you would also have to imagine the same information is available to push your ideas and desires as existing into its fullness, ready for you to access.

This information again is the inner mirror that should be reflected into your outer mirror as you connect and create relationships towards your desire that will represent itself in cycles of time.

The Energy Body

The energy body is a Universal body that expands from your body as represented by the formulation and placement of your relationships. Any type of action stemming from the people you are connected with or associated with, causes fluctuation in this body. This energy body acutely reflects your personal energy, but as I said earlier, it is also a way of playing the Universal energies much like playing musical instruments. This is a direct way of influencing the Universal energy that's tied directly to you.

This energy becomes a substantive energy that is set to provide towards your successes and accomplishments. This is not a religious notion. This is a fact of true existences based on the laws and scientific principals of the Universe. So it becomes highly important to align with the right people for right purposes. The Universe always provides the first move to put people in front of you that are right for you. When the mind becomes busy or directionless, we spend time missing our appointments instead of connecting with our appointments, which then leads to disappointment.

Energy is a gift. It is exacting. It is also highly directed. This is why we can depend on energy to do so much in our lives today. All that you see on your cell phone, PC tablets, television, and music players are directed energies. The Universe in the same way carries the energy of your desire and direction. Now you must connect and relate to people who carry that same energy.

The Universal Response Body

The Universal Response Body reflects your Emotional Body. Much in the same way the Energy Body works, the Universe is set to respond to your every desire, but this response is tied into your emotional system. What's unique about the living Universe, as it is an intricate part of your body, like your local emotional system, its movements are more laid out physically in response to a thought. The sun, which is a universal component, physically supplies the earth many benefits such as photosynthesis, vitamin D for the body, and energy for solar heating and electricity. In the same way, every physical thing in the Universe, including distant galaxies and star constellations are a physical supply to your direction.

Everything, whether consciously witnessed are not, is set to respond. You must really include in your main consciousness that there is more happening per every thought and action than you can ever begin to imagine. Let's look at it this way. The Universe is 98% hydrogen and helium. The rest of the known minerals comprise only 2% of physical matter. So when you set a desire, and just those two elements respond, 98% of your goal is complete at the onset of that thought. So the Universe in its entirety responds to your thinking and you fully have a Universal Response Body.

Your Completions Body

Your completions are completed on the onset of your thoughts. This is the point of significance. Accomplishment. A cycle started is a cycle completed. What must be done, is one must step into the cycles of his or her completions. If something is completed, then a mapping of that completion exists and cannot be measured by dates, but must measured by relationships. Here, the energy of what you want is considered. That map can be accessed by your inner mirror and witnessed in time, which is your outer mirror.

It is vital that your relationships follow the frequency, cycles, and the energy. When this happens you then experience a closing of distance and a deep since of significance.

Putting It All Together

Mind Body/Reflected Completions Body

1. Place a point of creative accomplishment as a your desire.

    a. Never make an individual your point of accomplishment.
    b. Give this point of creative accomplishment your attention.

2. Choose what you decide to see.

    a. If the energy of what you see or exchange with doesn't match your desire, change it.
    b. You have to consciously guard your perspective. Perspective is an energy.

Emotional Body/Reflected Universal Response Body

1. Practice your accomplishment until it becomes memory.

    a. Listen to music and videos that relate to your direction.
    b. Invest in materials and training from those who accomplished what you want.

2. Set your environment to speak to you your direction.

    a. Clear things that don't work.
    b. Go to places consistently that are related to what you want.

3. Chose relationships based on the sound that they are willing to invest in you.

    a. People around you must vocally agree with your direction.
    b. Eliminate people who do not keep their word.

Relationships Accounts Body/Reflected Energy Body

1. Have people around you that take specific action and contribute towards your accomplishment.

    a. You have to be vigilant about eliminating non-contributors.
    b. Love is never words only.

2. Take measurement of what people contribute to your end-goals.

    a. People must be intimately involved. You shouldn't feel a distance.
    b. Treat your directions like a corporation and make action toward your direction a requirement. Anything else will be a waste of time.

Time Body/Reflected Spirit Body

1. Turn the cycle of what's created within you over to individuals that have cooperating energy.

    a. Use the Credit List to determine and qualify who these people are.
    b. Remember each person is like the ground where you plant a seed in order to complete a cycle.

2. Take measurement of production points within your set cycles.

    a. Time as mandated by Universal energy has marked points of production much similar to seasons and how seasons work. A person's energy is equated to these marked points. Make sure that your connections produce within these marked points.

b. Time will always open up your marked points and cycles to you just like seasons. Know them before you get there.

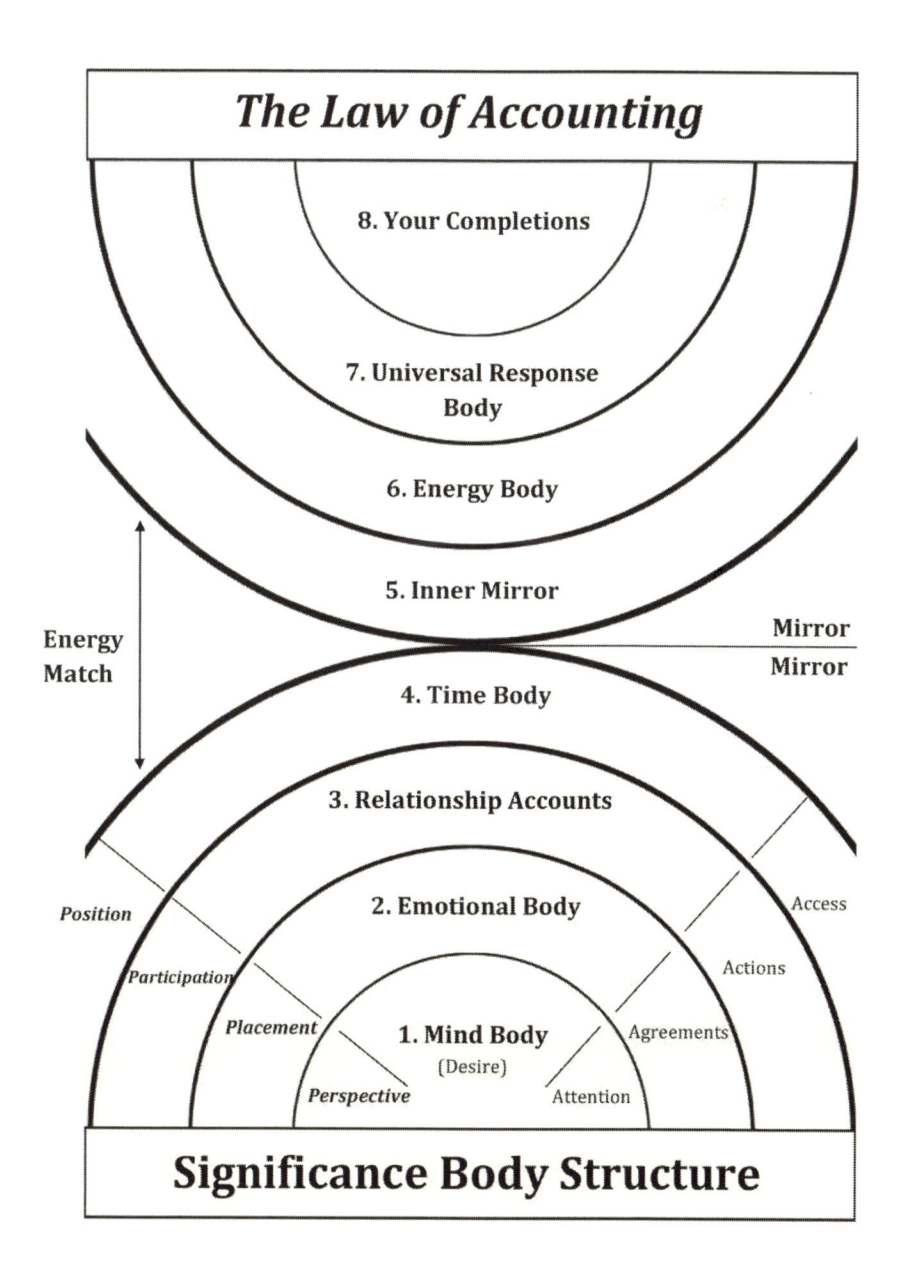

The Law of Accounting

- 8. Your Completions
- 7. Universal Response Body
- 6. Energy Body
- 5. Inner Mirror
- 4. Time Body
- 3. Relationship Accounts
- 2. Emotional Body
- 1. Mind Body (Desire)

Energy Match

Mirror / Mirror

Position, Participation, Placement, Perspective, Attention, Agreements, Actions, Access

Significance Body Structure

Rules of Engagement

Chapter 3

Rules of Engagement

Every part of your 8-part full body existence within the Law of Accounting is intricately tied into how you set your subsequent relationships according to the law. All of these relationships from your business, personal, family, intimate and the like, must point towards your desire and must feed into your life's purpose. Most miss the opportunity to take the time to measure the strengths of their relationships, and then never realize that whenever there is a sense of insignificance, it is a result of having little concentration on their life desires and then basing their relationships on that desire. With this, people engage other people without purpose, hoping that purpose will arise after the fact. So here are some strategies and tools for the rules of engagement:

First, understand that people operate and approach life based on 8 levels or strata of intelligence. They are as follows:

1. Primal
2. Basic
3. Advanced
4. Coordinal
5. Creative
6. Innovative
7. Clairvoyant Constructive
8. All Knowing

When engaging someone it is good to know and have an awareness of the following:

1. Know the strata of intelligence of the individual you are engaging.
2. Determine your own personal intelligence strata within your approach.

3. Determine the energy level of the connections you share based on the intelligences.
4. Intelligence will determine an individual's potential for contribution and then their ability to contribute to your cause.

Again, there are basically 8 strata intelligence levels that you have to consider from two different angles.

1. What is your level or point of intelligence?
2. What is the level of intelligence of the individual or individuals you plan to engage or currently engaging?

Here are the eight levels, their characteristics, and their sense of government, their energy, and how their energy ties in for you to consider.

Intelligence Level	Characteristics	Sense of Government	Energy
Primal	Sees from a point of survival Hindsight Underemployed/Unemployed	Environment	Little or No Energy Leaching type
Basic	See things based on instruction Basic sight Worker – Managed	Civic Law	Low Energy Aligning
Advanced	See things as given Insight Worker – Self-starter	Religion/God	Average Energy Manageable
Coordinal	See things in order On-sight Managerial	Self Organization	Consistent Energy Maintaining
Creative	See things different Foresight Director	Self Awareness	High Energy Contributive
Innovative	See things new Insight to foresight C-Level Executive	What's New	Very High Energy Investing
Clairvoyant Constructive	See things ahead Foresight to insight Owner/Operator	What's Ahead	Extreme Energy Constructive
All Knowing	Sees all things Cleat sight	Nothing	Greatest Energy Intimate

Every human on earth has all 8 intelligence faculties, but one is generally dominate. If your primary approach is from a lower intelligence stratum, you can sometimes through inspiration, connect with a higher stratum of intelligence. You are designed to operate at the highest level, but most are still maturing from lower strata points. Yes. Moving from strata to strata becomes a matter of maturing or growing to new levels and creating the relationships that foster that growth.

1. What is your level of intelligence as you set your desires and then approach your desires?

So first, when it comes to determining your dream, direction, or desire, you can use this chart to determine your own level of approach. From which standpoint of intelligence do approach your own strategies? You might want to approach your dreams, direction, and desires from a creative level or above and not from the lower three levels.

2. What is the level of intelligence strata of the individuals you plan to engage or engaging?

To assist with this, you can also use the chart to determine what type persons you are making your connections with. If you find yourself in a non-creative space or a non-productive space, find some creative individuals or higher to exchange with.

The greater the level of intelligence you operate on, the greater the energy is around you. The primal level invokes the lowest energy setting. If you are trying to push your ideas to the next level, you wouldn't do well by connecting to individuals who operates on the primal strata. They would have little to contribute to your endeavors

Again you want to first determine who you are. What is your intelligence approach? Then you want to consider the intelligence strata of who you're involved with.

Here is how to identify another's strata:

1. Listen to their language.
2. Pay attention to their results.
3. Check their environments.
4. Monitor to their current relationships.

Once you have determined a person's intelligence strata, it can become crystal clear as to how your results with them will turn out. This helps with giving yourself an advanced notice on your end results. Many have engaged individuals, only to find out in the end that things did not turn out as intended. Knowing the intelligence strata gives you the power to know your ends in the beginning.

Examples of using the Stratum:

If you want to keep things straight and in order, connect to a co-ordinal individual.

If you're looking for new ideas, connect to an innovator.

If you are an innovator, you will have issues of moving forward with someone who is consistently primal.

A creative stratum would hardly mix in with a coordinal stratum. The creativity, which requires some risk, would irritate someone who is coordinal in nature.

If you are a coordinal, for example, it would be hard to estimate future moves without precise plans being laid out. With this, it might be good to connect with an innovator who doesn't require such stringency.

An advanced intelligence would have a hard time connecting to with a clairvoyant intelligence, because the advanced would need to hear from God before making a decision, were as the clairvoyant intelligence can see it already.

A coordinal intelligence, for example, couldn't connect without the vision having some type of organization, a primal intelligence wouldn't care, so a conversation with a innovative intelligence might be useless with either.

Many times we are completely unaware of compatibility when it comes to the intelligence strata. This is seen, for example, when a individual is clairvoyant, which means he or she can naturally see things ahead of time, this clairvoyant will find themselves having a hard time explaining their vision to someone who is primal, basic, advanced, or coordinal. But you can connect with a coordinal to organize something for you, an advanced intelligence to pray for you, and a basic intelligence to do some work.

The Gift of Measurement

The next rule of engagement is to take measurement. I'll break down the word measure into two parts:

Me-Assure

The quickest way to insignificance is ignorance. Living life for granted. I am sure by now, you must realize that significance isn't derived based on people's treatment of you, but by you taking responsibility to take some type of action when things are not right. To do this, you must be acutely aware of potential unfortunate situations that might arise. You do not have to wait until "after-the-fact" before gaining knowledge of something that's not going to work. Here is another key or rule along with the 8 Intelligence Strata that can clue you in to potential. Here are the 4 Points of Measurement:

1. Measured Motifs   The 1st Relationship Set
2. Measured Money   The 2nd Relationship Set
3. Measure Moments   The 3rd Relationship Set
4. Measured Monuments   The 4th Relationship Set

The 1st Relationship Set is Measured Motifs.

Motif is taking note to what's repeating. Many find themselves stuck in rut. Their experience in life is void of growth. They live the same thing over and over again with no idea of how to make the results of their next move different. Well, I will clue you in. When something needs to change you must change the energy.

The energy of your results matches or is congruent to the energy of your relationships. If there is no growth in relational habits, then there will be no growth in your ability to accomplish. Individuals who perpetuate a sense of insignificance in you are the same individuals who have little to offer you. The problem is measurement of the relationship is not taken, ignored, or simply taken for granted.

If something needs to change, you must change the energy.

You have to have a sense of expectancy from everyone around you. If there is no performance or underperformance, you have the make the bold decision to do something different. Otherwise you will repeat the same crap over and over again. Life is designed to repeat or to cycle, but at each point of repetition, you must find yourself on a different plateau.

Please do not underestimate the power of your plateau. A plateau signifies that you have gone as far as you can go. What people generally do not do here, is reach for another platform, but just repeat the same thing over again. They don't know how to mark enough is enough; they don't know how to mark "we have gone as far as we can go"; they don't know how to mark "our time is up"; they don't know how to mark "we have reached a plateau". Plateaus are signals to move up and not repeat the same thing. You must take measurements. The energy of every level of accomplishment has been predetermined for you.

Success is always guaranteed, you only have to require the people around you to extend into you with a sense of guarantees. This provides the environment of always seeing what's next, seeing new levels, and locking into your completions beforehand.

The 2nd Relationship Set is Measured Money.

Money is your ability to trust what's out there that is right for you. Not only must you measure people's behavior towards you, but you must also be able to measure the results of that behavior, or what I call your personal paydays. There is always a result. You can never take for granted the level of a person's consideration towards you. Practicing any level of ignorance towards your self is practicing poverty. Remember, practice builds memory in your body. So there must be certain things that should be absolutely unacceptable to you when the exchange is not right.

You can never take for granted the level of a person's consideration towards you.

All energy is money. If your drove up to a drive-thru menu and ordered a full meal, pulled up to the first window and paid for a full meal, then drove up to the second window and only received fries; you don't go back around and try again and make another payment, hoping that it will come out right the next time? No. You make the correction on the spot. When individuals are short-changed in their relationships, they simply try again. But it must be realized, that just within the act of trying again, you are trying again at a loss. This is not trusting in what's right for you. Your trust has shifted over to the individual's capability to do right. So most try to change the person versus changing direction. A corporation never extends toleration to what's not right by investing in trust of a person changing. They fire what's wrong and hire what's right.

The 3rd Relationship Set is Measured Moments.

Pay attention to your moments and how people are contributing to your moments. Herein lie 2 more Points of Attention and the 12 Points of Significance. Let's first look at the 3rd and 4th attention.

The Third Attention

The third attention happens in the seen world of completions. It is taking stock in your successes and making sure that you are reaching your end goals. It is being aware of the things completed and uncompleted. You must decide by making precise moves towards directions that are set by you and then put in the time to develop what you have decided on without being distracted with things and people who have nothing to do with where you are going. It is your ability to produce. These are second stages of affirmation. Here you have to give heightened attention to what's done by you and the people around you.

The Forth Attention

The forth attention happens in the seen world of growth. Growth is duplicating your efforts effortlessly based on the confirming things and people around you. It is being aware of and taking stock in whether or not you are stuck in one place or stuck on the same level, or whether or not you are constantly and consistently moving forward and gaining new heights. You must be in a state of movement and growth at all times, and then deal with people who are doing the same for themselves and towards you. This is the basis of progression. Here you have to give heightened attention to your progress.

12 Points of Significance

Your economy starts with your relationship with others. Again, the definition of money is your ability to trust and engage what's right for you. Your ability to do this this affects your capabilities to move to new levels. As you complete one level, or reach a plateau, the next level of accomplishment will automatically and faithfully be presented.

Whenever you have been rested one level, the next level is already there waiting for your systemic aggregation of relationships to bring what you're looking for into reality or into the reality of your desired experience - good experience. True intimacy is not about having to think, because your relationship "machine" is so responsive to you, that the difference between thinking and manifesting becomes seamless. Here you are living versus surviving. When you don't reach for what's inside you to determine your significance, you then reach for things and people outside of yourself to do this job in order make you feel your significance. Your significance then is at the mercy of other people's behavior verses it being designed by you and then having other people coming into agreement to those designs.

Just as the Universe contains 12 main energy structures that can be considered as frequencies or music notes, you have what I call 12 main entry points or gates to your well being. These points are energetic in nature and must be monitored for healthy exchanges. Consider yourself as an entity with 12 gates. Each of the gates is crucial to your personal economy. These gates are the entry points to your soul and cannot be left to willy-nilly exchanges with others. Missing any one of these energy points will allow a great sense of insignificance to loom. Learning these 12 points of significance gives you an acute monitoring system to gage your relationships and to make sure they are on par with your personal health and wealth. Here are the 12 points:

1
(To Be Viewed)
The Investment of seeing and knowing a person

2
(To Be Comprehended)
The Investment of understanding a person

3
(To Be Engaged)
The Investment of active commitment

4
(To Be Praised)
The Investment of vocal affirmation of the good

5
(To Be Believed)
The Investment of trust

6
(To Be Prioritized)
The Investment of making one special

7
(To Be Enriched)
The Investment of provision

8
(To Be Advanced)
The Investment of pushing one forward

9
(To Be Rewarded)
The Investment of active recognition

10
(To Be Exalted)
The Investment of one's self into another

11
(To Be Increased)
The Investment of addition

12
(To Be Doubled)
The Investment of multiplication

You need all of these investments to have a complete sense of being. Again, these are energy entry points and they all stem from your relationships. These 12 points can serve as a checklist to your exchanges. Here are the details:

1
(To Be Viewed)
The Investment of seeing and knowing a person.

- To know a person as in their habits, favorite things, concerns etc.

- To be concerned and having a person's back based on what you see in them.

- See, recognize, and care for one's issues.

Everyone needs someone to see and know who they are.

2
(To Be Comprehended)
The Investment of understanding a person.

- Understanding of one's issues.

- Willing to take in right information concerning a person.

- Agreement and right action towards that understanding of the person.

Everyone has a need to be understood.

3
(To Be Engaged)
The Investment of active commitment.

- Physical connection.

- Partnership and unification.

- Two way exchange or communication.

Everyone has a need to be touched in some way.

**4
(To Be Praised)
The Investment of vocal affirmation of the good.**

- Recognition and hearing about good attributes.

- Complimentary in nature towards a person.

- Approvals of ideas, thoughts, visions...etc.

Everyone has a need to hear something good about them.

**5
(To Be Believed)
The Investment of trust.**

- Take a position based on concerns verbalized, or character exuded.

- Action oriented belief qualified by action oriented support.

- Taking responsibility and acting on a person's behalf based believing in them.

Everyone has a need to be trusted and believed in.

**6
(To Be Prioritized)
The Investment of making one special.**

- Acute attention in certain situations and areas.

- Putting things aside in recognition of the other.

- Allowing a person from time to time to be the most important.

Everyone has the need to feel number one sometimes.

**7
(To Be Enriched)
The Investment of provision.**

- Bringing gifts or supplies not associated with earning.

- Sharing your personal substance.

- Making sure a person's needs are met.

Everyone has a need to receive.

**8
(To Be Advanced)
The Investment of pushing one forward.**

- Progressing one's effort by means of time and efforts.

- Providing leadership in your area of expertise to advance the cause of another.

- To give an effort in setting a situation or circumstance right.

Everyone has a need to be mentored or pushed forward.

**9
(To Be Rewarded)
The Investment of recognition.**

- To provide substance in recognition of what someone has invested in you.

- Physical substance given in appreciation for efforts made.

- Thank you and appreciation outside of verbal affirmation.

Everyone has a need to be appreciated in a tangible way.

10
(To Be Exalted)
The Investment of one's self into another.

- Time spent in all areas of emotional investments.

- Giving a sense of place based on your presence.

- The gift of yourself that lifts a person to another level, give status or empowers.

Everyone has a need to feel another's presence that builds their own presence.

11
(To Be Increased)
The Investment of addition.

- To empower, enhance or enable in any way.

- To see then add in a positive way time, effort, or substance.

- To be an extension for someone where someone comes short.

Everyone has a need to be completed by the investment of another's effort and partnership.

12
(To Be Doubled)
The Investment of multiplication.

- The experience of results.

- Results that lead to more results.

- Results that give a sense of place, home, completeness.

Everyone has a need to grow by the investment of another's effort or partnership.

All 12 are contributions to your well-being. These contributions are ongoing energy lines that affect your thoughts, your movements, and your accomplishments. Furthermore, these 12 points are the very construct of your significance and must be well managed as well as not taken for granted. The reason being, your personal energy balance works in tandem with the 12 energy houses that govern the universe. How people treat you, engage you, and how people see you has both a local affect on your personal existence, but it also has a universal affect as well as all things are tied into one system.

In given situation, as you are relating, you must turn the 12 points into questions such as:

1. Can this person see who I am?

2. Does this person understand me?

3. Does this person engage what I'm trying to accomplish?

4. Am I getting praise or affirmation from this individual?

5. Does this person believe me? Does this person believe in what I'm doing?

6. Am I being prioritized? Does this person put me first?

7. Are you meeting my needs?

8. Is this person pushing me to the next level?

9. Does this person appreciate me?

10. Does this person spend sufficient time with me that makes a difference in my progress?

11. Am I empowered by this person?

12. Can I see something in this person that I see in myself?

As you go through the 12 Points of Significance, you can create your own questions. Write down a list of people you know including family, friends, lovers, business relationships etc. Which of the 12 points do they contribute towards you? Use the questions to monitor their level of participation in your life. What is their energy contribution? What extends outside of our self is commercial in every sense of the word. The energy that extends outside of our self is commercial. These 12 points are points of commerce.

You are a local point of commerce.

Every marketplace in existence from the trading post in the country lands, to the malls and shopping centers in the major urban centers, to the major world trade centers, to the world's stock exchanges are merely advanced systems of commerce that extends from some individual's local point of commerce. Every major corporation was first a corporation that existed within someone in the form of an idea. This idea was balanced and then expressed through his immediate relationships. This is why money is a matter of your personal exchanges and not physical currency. Physical currency is only a mirror of the true commercial state of your 12 energy points or 12 points of significance.

The 4th Relationship Set is Measured Monuments.

Monuments are your points of accomplishments. I want to delve a little deeper into the differences between an initiating idea and accomplishing that idea. First, there is no real difference between an initiating idea and accomplishing that idea, only a difference in the state of existence. You can view the concept of these states much like air, water, and ice. They are all the exact same substance, but the state is influenced by the energy of its environment or the arrangement of this energy.

Everything you want to accomplish is accounted before you. But you can set the energy of your environment via the 12 points. This in turn will determine your accomplishments or the state of your accomplishments, which actually exist at the inception of your thoughts. What I want to enforce here is that significance is not derived from your relationships as most would think, but significance is derived from your relationships that are in tandem with your desires, which means you must have the desire before the relationship. Here you cannot blame people for their treatment of you, but you must take responsibility for structuring your relationships around what you want. Measure the monuments that extend from these relationships.

Universal Parenting Energy

Chapter 4

Universal Parenting Energy

What I want to do here is further prove the presence of your accomplishments by introducing you to Universal Parenting Energy or UPE. Again, what you accomplish in life is of upmost importance. Your ability to grow from stage to stage, from plateau to plateau, and from platform to platform, mirrors the entirety of how the Universe is unfolding. So to understand the unfolding of your desires and the states of your desires we will look into the construct of the Universal Parenting Energy.

Just like a parent, I want you to consider this energy as the energy in which you derive your own existence and a subsequent nurturing energy that oversees your growth points much like a parent. For every type of energy in existence there is parent energy. Now I equate the Law of Accounting with the Anatomy of Significance, but I really want you to get a clearer understanding of what the Law of Accounting is about.

The word "accounting" signifies a financial consideration. All things in the universe are financial in nature because energy is always in a constant state of exchange. Energy is also in a constant state of provision and is fully aware within itself what it is providing for. So the Universe within itself carries a parenting energy, which I call Universal Parenting Energy or UPE. Understanding UPE will clue you into how all that you every want is counted before you as a guarantee. You then can use the Law of Accounting to begin to structure your life and your relationships to gain access to your own accomplishments.

First let's look the parenting aspect of UPE. I want to use a case of adoption to make this clear. An adopted child before being adopted had many elements of assurance that was missing. Once adopted, these assurances came into existence. What do I mean by this? Once adopted, there is a new expectancy of support that is acquired. This child can now fully expect to be fed every day. His or her future events are looked after. When there is a need, mommy and daddy will take care of it. There is a sense of expected provision that will remain well beyond high school as well as college graduation.

The provision of an adopted child in general doesn't have to be asked for or chased after. So in a great sense, because of now having parents, their life is accounted for. The same goes for children that are children by birth. Their life is accounted for by a provisional parenting energy. Everyone, every human has a parenting energy that exists outside of his or her biological parents. This is the Universal Parenting Energy. This energy works in the exact same way when it comes to accounting for your accomplishments.

The moment you think a thought, generate an idea, a desire, or set a destination, you must first be fully conscious of the fact that that thought, idea, desire or destination is a universal birthing process that provides the first state of existence. This why I say, the moment you think of something, it exists in its entirety. This is not a spiritual notion that needs to be hinged on faith and belief. It is an energetic fact. When you run on the premises of spiritualizing your dream, you distance yourself from realizing your productive capability. Think of what you want to accomplish from a point of factual existence and not from a point of "spiritual" access wherein you have to practice some type of ritual or observance to access your own success.

The day you say you want something or more so, the day you think of it, what you want becomes an energetic fact immediately. It is an energy frequency that spans the entirety of the universe. The knowledge of what you want is now contained in the energy mix of the Universe. I am amazed how we can believe in the existence of a voice on a cell phone that can speak to you from thousands of miles away, but then reduce the idea that your thoughts have the same frequenetic properties. Therefore, we take our thoughts for granted or we don't assess value to our thoughts.

Just like a cell phone frequency, radio frequency, or a satellite frequency is governed by laws within the universe, so is your thought frequencies governed accordingly. More accurately your every thought is parented by UPE. What does this mean? The Universe, containing the greater energy structure, which models every point of your accomplishment, and which is the energy pattern that precedes your thoughts and wants, your thoughts and wants then can only be birthed out of accomplishment and cannot be birthed out of what is to be accomplished. So to accomplish something becomes a foregone conclusion once you think it. There is energy, and then there is parenting energy. The Universal Parenting Energy is the completion of your thoughts, dreams, desires, wants, and destinations.

We must no longer leave faith and belief to mysticism, but begin to measure and note the provided energy constructs that are placed here for us to count on, therefore is the need for the Law of Accounting. We run our satellites, cell phones, TV's, I-pads, computers, and Mp3 players off of these same guaranteed laws. Now it's time to run ourselves off these same universal laws when it comes to human concerns, and not make them a spiritual or mystic phenomenon where only a few can attain based on strengic practices, strenuous exercises, and ongoing search for truth. In the mist of stretching towards an outer world for guidance, our intellect suffers as we neglect to manage the energies given to us, which in turn causes our significance to suffer.

So we have this Universal Parenting Energy, which is part of your local body. The energy of this body is made up of the last four structures of your Significance Body.

1. Your Completions
2. Your Universal Response Body
3. Your Universal Energy Body
4. Your Inner Mirror

You might want to go back and read on these four body parts to bring to memory the elements of these four body parts. Remember these four body parts mirror your first four body parts.

1. Your Mind Body
2. Your Emotional Body
3. Your Relationship Body
4. Your Time Body or Your Outer Mirror

The last four are unseen energy structures, but it serves as the Universal Parenting Energy to what is seen. This is where all you could ever want and desire is strictly accounted for and guaranteed. The first four body parts; the mind, the emotional, the relationship, and time are the privilege of acting in, choosing in, and participating within mirrored processes, but done within the experience of experience. The Universe can only respond, mankind can experience. We are created to experience. To experience is to know life. The Universal Parenting Energy provides the structure for experience, just like a parent provides the structure for their children's experience.

Stemming out of the Universal Parenting Energy are the 12 initial house or energy frequencies provided for the basis of experience.

We can mirror these houses as they create an energy mix towards our accomplishments by first being able to tune an ear to what the Universe is playing into your personal atmosphere. How do you know the tune? Quite simple. You wrote it. The greatest fear that you and I can possess is the fear of our own success, which is the fear of our own sound and the fear of our own desires. So we rest in relationships that hold a diminished capacity for comfort, which goes against our own progression.

As these 12 vortexes sound into reality, you must take the 12 Points of Significance and align them to the sound of your accomplishment. This begins in the exercises that influence the mind, and then the structure of the chemicals called emotions that are built within your body based on your agreements.

If a person in your life represents the wrong sound, it is at that point you will miss entirely the guaranteed sound of the Universal Parenting Energy. That is why your subsequent actions aren't provided for. Have you ever engaged an individual over and over again and nothing changes, nothing grows, nothing is accomplished, but you keep hoping it will?

So;

1. You decide what you want
2. The Parenting Energy provides you with the frequency of your accomplishments
3. You tune your relationships using the 12 Points of Significance accordingly
4. Time provides you with your respective states of existence for experience
5. If you need help, your Inner Mirror will guide you
6. Your Outer Mirror of time will always tell you where you are
7. Make honest adjustments when necessary
8. You will then become the model of accomplishment for someone else, a Universal Parenting Energy.

Practice Your Personal Frequencies.

Your mind operates on frequencies, and the practice of these frequencies is built within your body as memory. You must be vigilant to remain awake over and above the frequencies that you do not desire. Knowing and monitoring your behavior as it is reflected from the 8 Intelligence Stratus will clue you into frequency management; primal and basic intelligence providing the lowest, and clairvoyant and all knowing intelligence providing you with the highest. You can also use the same strata points of forming your relationships by determining the level wherein you are being approached.

Finally, control the investments going out and the investments coming in using the 12 Points of Significance. Never leave your self-worth at the mercy of someone else's behavior, but at the helm of your own design. The core of the Universal Parenting Energy is like an apple seed, an apple, and an orchard of apples; the apple and the orchard is contained in the seed and its production capabilities extends out into infinity by law. For every seed, there is an orchard, more apples, and then more seeds. The history of what is present in the seed extends all the ways back to the beginning of existence, and this history fully supports the presence of the current seed's intent all the way into the future as it concerns the seed's ability to produce.

Anything that you desire is supported by that same historical energy and you are capable of producing anything you want in life as long as a future exists. You are privileged to carry within you what's next.

Sex. Is it Good for Business?

You can't really talk about relationships without talking about sex. Viewpoints on sex are primarily shaped by culture. The second highest influence on sexual viewpoints is religion and spiritual beliefs. Sex holds a special place in evolutionary development and it is a powerful act that impacts more components of the psyche and the body simultaneously than any other act or substance. It is the source of our very existence, but yet the least considered when it comes to open discussion. Surprisingly, the totality of sexuality is not a major classroom topic within our educational system and one of the hardest topics for parents here in America to discuss with their children. In other countries, sex and sexuality is central to the countries culture and belief system.

Sex within itself is most fascinating for many reasons. It involves so much activity from a physical standpoint, yet having an equal impact and involvement from a psychological standpoint. It affects the brain and brainwave activity, the nervous system, your emotional composition, which is the release and flow of chemicals in the body; it affects the electrical composition of the body and blood flow.

Some consider sex to be a singular activity of intercourse. Other's consider sex to involve a series of activities which include foreplay or some form of touch. Actually touch within itself and the capacity to touch is what set humans apart from other species. Touch is what drove our evolutionary development past mundane existences to advanced life forms.

The Luxury of Touch

I can confidently say that it is the phenomenon of touch that drives all human activity and development. Touch can easily be considered as the physical side of significance. If you can for moment think of the five senses; when it comes to hearing, there are species that have a heightened sense of hearing. There are species that have a heightened sense of smell, sight, and taste; but touch is a human capability that puts us at the top of the evolutionary chain. I would dare say, that all of our advancement stems from touch and the communication it offers.

Let's go back to the newborn. A newborn that is born wanting. A newborn that is born receiving. It has been proven that a newborn going untouched will die after a short while. Touch is a bodily activator. A child who receives little touch will grow up with a sadistic mentality and live a scorned existence. A child who is touched in a wrong way or inappropriately lives with lifelong scars that is emotional crippling. A wrong touch can disable a human being for life.

On the opposite side of the spectrum, touch has been used as tool for healing diseases and bringing a secure sense of comfort. It is the experience of comfort that comes from a touch that can bring on an immediate sense of significance. There is a unique sense of communication that is accomplished through touch. Touch is the highest form of experience because of its sense of return.

What makes us human is the ability to experience what returns. Awareness of our own existence by what presents itself to us for experience is what life is. This is the core question of significance. Am I alive? The only way I can know is by what gives itself to me.

The Gift of Attention

Accomplishment is great and offers a sense of being as you reach certain milestones, but attention is something that is deliberately chosen by another to invest in you. The greatest of these investments is touch.

The sense of that experience alone is phenomenal. As I said earlier, there are four senses that make us alive, it is touch that makes us human. To really understand this, you must understand what sex is.

Some can have intercourse without having sex, and sex can be experienced without intimacy. What we are primarily talking about here is union, but more accurately, how we unite. As pointed out in the 12 Points of Significance our unions should come with certain presentations and expectations. The most core form of uniting is sex. Nothing comes into existence without union. You can almost say that our Universe is sex. The implication of this is extreme. To understand this can open the mind to boundless possibilities because the sexual union can become the foundation as to how we are educated.

In America, accomplishment and attainment is generally at the core of why we do things. There is nothing wrong with this at all, but the approach of accomplishment and attainment has more a ting of singularity of consciousness versus a consciousness of what potentially can come from a union. The core of biology is reproduction, and in most species reproduction is done via some type of union. In most species the union is a result of primal needs, but in humans, unions are chosen and can be chosen by design. In this choosing, some have to hunt for mating opportunities and others garner given attention that leads to the same.

A newborn, again, cries for attention and then receives attention, but attention given based on the consciousness of need by the other without the newborn having to cry for it is powerful. There is a sense of significance that does stem from the wanting, crying, and then receiving. There is a much greater significance that is experienced if a need is met without a cry, because it is personally assessed that this individual has a great sense, awareness, and consciousness of me, and they acted on it.

Attention given is powerful, because attention given is based on having a consciousness of the other. This essentially says that you exist, but yet you also exist in the mind of the other. This is a natural increase in existence. A person here gets an expanded sense of existence, which is good for significance and the psychological appetite. Imagine having a favorite ice cream and you having the ability to express to the other that you would like some of that ice cream, and the other then proceeds to make it available to you. That feels good. Now imagine the other without you expressing or even asking for the ice cream presenting you with the ice cream you like just because they were just thinking about you. Now you have a greater sense of existence, because you also exist in the mind of the other.

Attention is that powerful. Attention expands existence. This is the greatest source and gift of creation ever; what you create in your mind about the other and what the other creates in their mind about you. With this, a person can be expanded into infinity, but it takes the other to accomplish this. A good number of people have lost their sense of the other or even the need for the other because of past experiences in how they have been treated. Even in this culture, accomplishment is a point of singular processing because people have the need to protect and preserve their sense of self because of past damages, so there is a hesitation in connecting. Some even form a lifestyle of staying mildly disassociated to chronically disassociated. This is a great misfortune and a lot of people have no clue on how to heal from this.

Hopefully you understand that attention expands the existence of the other, and so the ability give attention is a gift. Touch is the most significant version of attention. Sexual intercourse is the powerful form of expression and touch. When sex is performed correctly, you can get a great sense of expansion. You experience this expansion in the moment. Some religions and spiritual practices promote that abstinence from sex can lead to a heightened sense of spirituality. This is funny as hell because they couldn't even get here in order to promote chastity without their parents having sex.

The Maturing of Connection

With sex being the deepest form of connection, you must understand that the meaning of sex is still maturing over time. Our connections, how we connect, and our ability to connect is still maturing as time progresses. How we live today, how we connect, and how we have sex today is more advanced than earlier civilizations, but not much. . How we live today, how we connect, and how we have sex today will mature into higher forms in the distant future.

What happens in the body primarily doesn't have to mature when it comes to sex, but what sex means and understanding the power that it holds can mature. Sex is a primal act of connection, but sex within itself is not specifically tied to the primal. I consider sex as a primal act because of its history and because of the fact that it is a common act among the entirety of human behavior. Not everybody can build a building, not everybody can calculate algorithms that drive the markets, not everybody can build a computer; not everybody can bake a cake, play golf, drive a car, swim, eat hot sauce, dance, play the guitar, do electrical work, fly an airplane, fly in an airplane, water ski, become a doctor, practice law, teach a class, milk a cow, fry chicken; but most individuals can and will have sex. Sex is dietary in nature. It is a human calling that pushes from your body without much promotion. The need for sex and touch is equivalent to the need to eat and go to the bathroom.

Sex historically started in the primal, and primarily remains in the primal even though humans have advanced in so many other areas. In many cases sex remains an area wherein some can fall back into the primal to escape advanced life existences for a minute. But what if we could advance how we have sex and how we choose to have sex?

Sex can be had without attention given. This could be the most dangerous form of sex, because the primary goal is for only one person to walk away with a sense of accomplishment, the other is left with a sense of incompletion. This is the most primal form of sex. "I'm coming to get what I want. I am coming to cum". One of the most advanced forms of sex currently is when a significant amount of attention accompanies the sex. This allows for more parts of your body and bodily experiences to be involved. This type of sex is accompanied with a lot of touch nad a higher sense of awareness of the other.

What is being said here is that I have you on my mind, which gives you a great sense of personal expansion. Imagine a sexual experience that is accompanied by expansion. Your body reads this expansion. If your body reads this expansion, you become the expansion from the attention given. I'm not just talking mentally; you are literally expanded physiologically during this type of sex and connection. What's amazing here is that this expansion immediately becomes the archetype for other types and dimensions of expansions that you want to accomplish. This is because with the right sexual experience, additional life is built into the body, and with humans being natural producers more life is experienced outside of the body accordingly. Historically, amongst Jews and Africans sex prowess was a sign of vitality within one's ability to produce wealth.

Is Sex Good for Business?

The bottom line of sex is financial in nature. As stated earlier, life is a composite of energies. We are only privileged to arrange these energies for our own experience and for the experience of others. Your emotions are comprised of a composition of nerves within the nervous system, nerve endings and chemicals. Sex activates all of this including how your blood flows. Sex is a power act to the body and has so many implications beyond primal connecting. It is the greatest initial energy exchange the can have a ripple affect universal wide.

With this, I say, sex is business. It always is and has been, but we are scared of that word "business". We generally only assign the word "business" to a corporate structure or some form of marketing and commerce, but never really realize that every move you make is commercial in nature. This is why so many individuals do not manage their relationships, less known, manage their sex. These are simply left willy-nilly to the primal.

I always wondered after having an amazing sexual experience if the feeling of that experience can be expanded and extended into the rest of life's moments. Come on…orgasms can be great, but what if we could live at the height of that orgasm continuously and consistently? What if there is something greater beyond the orgasm? Truly an orgasm can give a sense of peering into something more. Life is about more and most people who are in business experience more. Successful business-persons are great at their exchanges, which leaves them more in the end.

If you really break it down, sex should always leave you with more in the end, but you really cannot have more in the end if the person you are having sex with does not sufficiently have you on their mind and in their mind. You really have to sufficiently exist in them before they can move your bodily functions to the necessary levels for a heightened sexual experience. Even in sex, as an exchange is taking place on the most basic of levels, exchanges are also being made in the most intricate ways on so many other levels and dimensions. To become more conscious of these exchanges will mature our sexual experiences.

So here, much like in a business, you have to be smart in your sexuality. Many people practice poverty within their sexual practices. Many people are being robbed blind by the individuals they are having sex with. Primal sex can be a hotbed of a lifetime of disasters, especially when you know a person is no good, but something is driving you to mate with them. That's not a problem with them and their behavior; it is a problem with you and your choices. There is a belief, mainly because of the ideal of pursuing a person, that some people are that last people on earth so you must make it work with them. Using the 8 Intelligence Strata can be a tool to help you to determine who you should connect with sexually.

Some may ask, if I am not getting sufficient attention from the person I "love", where do I find the person or how do I attract the person. Herein lies the problem, you do not find nor do you attract, you must wake up. It's a process of waking up. For every level on the intelligence strata there is an associated energy. When you are sleeping with or dating bozos, it simply means the frequency of your consciousness is running on that level. So you do not change the person, you change your mind. Remember it's about controlling the energy of what's around you.

A lot of folks search for what is right versus waking up to what is right. When you sleep at night, your brain operates at several different frequencies. In your awake state, your brain operate at several different frequencies also, but some of these frequencies are still lower sleep frequencies even though you are awake. In these states, we do stupid stuff and connect with unnecessary people. You can take the 8 Intelligence Strata and treat it as a frequency reader.

Let's get a quick reminder.

1. Primal
2. Basic
3. Advanced
4. Coordinal
5. Creative
6. Innovative
7. Clairvoyant Constructive
8. All Knowing

Sex is great practice for success. It is the best bodily training for good memory that leads to success. I will not mix my words here. All the sex scandals you hear about stem from this very notion of absolute fact. Presidents, senators, fortune 500 CEOs, great entrepreneurs, pastors and other great spiritual leaders were all found pushing and paying for more sex. I mean to the tune of thousands of dollars per hour. Why? Because successful sex sets a model for great business exchanges. In reality sex from the right person can swiftly move an individual from a primal consciousness to an innovative plus consciousness. They are left with more in those circumstances and then they can extend that "more" into everything else that they can do.

Because of the sexual restructuring of our mental attitudes, we gasp in shock at some of this behavior, when in reality sex has been the true source of success for thousands of years since man moved past the primal state. For men in general, good sex can solve and resolve any sense of aloneness, insignificance, depression, anxiety, and fear within seconds. A man touched the right way can almost become invincible in his forward movements and progressions. A simple touch can be many times more powerful than any prescribed or illegal drug. A woman given the right type of attention snaps into immediate health and her confidence and sense of security becomes unshakable.

So sex is great practice for all types of future benefits. It is a short cut to the memory of success that I discussed earlier. Sex has for thousands of years been practiced within the primal, and sex can be matured and experienced from a greater vantage point. So we must have the ability to respond to higher forms of existence and intelligence. What I learned is that in order to extend the experience of sex beyond the act, I must connect intimately with persons who have a greater ability to contain who I am in their consciousness. The 12 Points of Significance can help you with this. Otherwise, your experience will fall shortly after having sex.

Opening Up from the Cutoff

Most people have sex within a safety zone. As I mentioned earlier, because of past histories and due to the fact that sex can be a very emotional event, sex can be a distant consideration. It is amazing that when a person does open up and make intimate contact, that contact usually mirrors the past troubles and then over time that person turns out to be a disappointment. If you fall off a bicycle many times, it is hard to get back on the bike and ride again. So most would spend wide expanses of their lives wrestling with bike riding instead of learning how to drive a car. They experience heartaches simply because their connections have been primal and they deal with primal people, and then, so goes the energy. A bike carries one type of energy, a car holds a whole different type of energy. This can be resolved by making the leap into having sexual experiences with those who have a more advanced outlook on life.

It's amazing how some people have brilliant minds and are forward thinking and then check out of that space to have sex with an average Jane or Joe. It's like plugging the AC unit to your house into where the toaster is plugged in. Let the sparks fly. Let the sparks die. Sex is what we know how to do, even with very little training. Management of our sex is a whole other issue.

So how do you improve your sex life? There are a lot of tips and tricks that can add spice and everything nice to sex, but what I found out, is if a person is sufficiently conscious of you, what to do to give you satisfaction comes out of nowhere. A person who holds their partner in conscious regard, seemly knows all the right moves to make. This even stand true when it comes to sexual stamina. If you are thinking more on the individual and what you are adding to their life, your need to reach a sexual peak is diminished during the sexual experience and the enjoyment increases for them. You are busy providing, and the other is busy growing while taking in the fact that they are on your mind.

There is a more intense sexual experience higher on the intelligence stratum. We must grow to that because we will grow from that. Then require your intimate connections to provide you with points of significance as part of their engagement with you. You must grow in those 12, then the Universe itself will participate in all that you do.

1
(To Be Viewed)
The Investment of seeing and knowing a person

2
(To Be Comprehended)
The Investment of understanding a person

3
(To Be Engaged)
The Investment of active commitment

4
(To Be Praised)
The Investment of vocal affirmation of the good

5
(To Be Believed)
The Investment of trust

6
(To Be Prioritized)
The Investment of making one special

7
(To Be Enriched)
The Investment of provision

8
(To Be Advanced)
The Investment of pushing one forward

9
(To Be Rewarded)
The Investment of active recognition

10
(To Be Exalted)
The Investment of one's self into another

11
(To Be Increased)
The Investment of addition

12
(To Be Doubled)
The Investment of multiplication

This concludes this small body of work. Hope it works for you.

Made in the USA
San Bernardino, CA
04 May 2014